Made at Home

Made at Home

The food I cook for the people I love –
family recipes for every day.

Giorgio Locatelli

with Sheila Keating

Photographs by Lisa Linder

4th Estate • London

4th Estate
An imprint of HarperCollins*Publishers*
1 London Bridge Street
London SE1 9GF
www.4thEstate.co.uk

First published in Great Britain by
4th Estate in 2017

1 3 5 7 9 8 6 4 2

Design and art direction: BLOK
www.blokdesign.co.uk

Typeset by GS Typesetting

A catalogue record for this book is available
from the British Library

ISBN 978-0-00-810051-3

Printed and bound in Germany by Mohn Media
Mohndruck GMBH

MIX
Paper from
responsible sources
FSC
www.fsc.org   **FSC® C007454**

FSC™ is a non-profit international organisation
established to promote the responsible management of
the world's forests. Products carrying the FSC label are
independently certified to assure consumers that they
come from forests that are managed to meet the social,
economic and ecological needs of present and future
generations, and other controlled sources.

Find out more about HarperCollins and the
environment at www.harpercollins.co.uk/green

For Plaxy

The places I call home

Home means many things to me. Home is north London with my wife, Plaxy, and now grown-up 'kids', Jack and Margherita, who come and go but still expect to raid the fridge as soon as they walk through the door. When Plaxy and I are at home on our own, the meals we share are about simply cooked fish, vegetables and salads, and many of our favourite recipes are included here. But when Margherita was small, much of our cooking had to begin with something that she could eat, since shortly after she was born we discovered that she had an allergy to around 600 foods, especially fish, tomatoes and eggs. So for years we could never have fish or tomatoes in the kitchen, and ingredients like almonds would be kept in jars in separate labelled cupboards to keep her safe. We never wanted her to feel different, so we would always find a way of making something for her that looked like what everyone else was eating, even if the ingredients varied. But for me, that should always be at the heart of all home cooking: the idea that you adapt and change according to what you buy fresh that is in season, what you have in your cupboard and your fridge, and who you are cooking for.

Home, for me, is also Corgeno in Lombardy, northern Italy, where my whole family was involved with my uncle's restaurant, La Cinzianella, on the shore of Lake Comabbio, so my grandmother was in charge of the cooking in our house while my grandfather raised rabbits and chickens and grew vegetables in the garden. Many of the meals that my grandmother cooked, I still cook at home for my own family, and when I do, it is as if I am back in Corgeno with her and my grandad again.

According to the day of the week, we might have risotto with saffron, pasta with homemade passata, fish from the lake, and once a week fresh prawns; or stews, such as osso buco or my favourite, *spezzatino*, made with beef, potatoes and peas, according to whatever pieces of meat Stefanino, the village butcher, had kept for my grandmother.

When my elder brother, Roberto, and I would come home from school there would often be a soup made with my grandmother's broth and maybe a *scallopine* to follow: a sliver of pork, veal or chicken, encrusted in breadcrumbs from the big jar in the kitchen and fried. I still think that in a family environment, soup is very important. It is a great comfort food; it doesn't need so much planning, and you can make a potful and freeze some in a container for next time. If I get home late from the restaurant, or from filming, having tasted so many dishes during the course of the day, all I want is a simple soup to soothe and settle the stomach. Or a simple pasta.

I never tire of a plate of spaghetti with a brilliant tomato sauce, but I often think that while the great advantage of pasta is its familiarity, that is also its worst enemy, because we all have our one or two favourite recipes that we make over and over again, when actually a dish of pasta should reflect the changing seasons. It is a perfect medium for introducing kids to ingredients with different textures and flavours throughout the year.

My grandparents, who had been through the war, never lost the fear that there might come a day when there was no food – something that Jack and Margherita have no reason to understand – but in

Europe plentiful food has come at a certain cost to society. There is no doubt that we have to address the problems of eating too much sugar and salt, the way we have made food 'convenient' by packing it full of additives, our wastefulness, and the fact that we cannot go on extracting so much from the earth and emitting so many gases. But one huge step is to go back to the essence of home cooking – buying fresh ingredients, preparing them simply, enjoying them with your friends and family, and keeping anything you don't eat to transform into another meal – and that's it.

Home, too, is my restaurant, Locanda Locatelli, where I spend most of my waking hours with my other family, the team of chefs and front of house staff, many of whom have been with me for a long, long time. You have to look after the people you work with. Ever since I sat on a rubbish bin outside the kitchen of the Tour d'Argent restaurant in Paris where I worked long, long hours for a pittance, eating sausages at the end of the night, while inside the diners paid a small fortune for the famous classic French dishes we had made for them, I vowed that when I had my own restaurant, I would make sure that everyone ate well. So each day at 4.30p.m. everyone sits down together to eat something simple that we have made in the kitchen, because that is when you have the time to talk to people, share ideas and news, find out what is going on in their lives, if someone needs help with something or has a problem. Exactly like a family sharing a meal around the table at home. The two favourite meals are 'Italian' burger night on Tuesday, and pizza night on Saturday, when even those who are due to finish their shifts, or on a day off, seem to find a reason to stay behind or drop by! So those recipes are included in this book, too.

And now Plaxy and I have a second home perched on the edge of a cliff overlooking the sea in Puglia, a region we discovered and fell in love with after spending so many amazing summers across the water in Sicily. In the winter, it feels like you could be on Mars, with the rocky cliff falling away beneath you, but in spring and summer the water is a stunning blue and that is all you can see.

In London, I am spoilt by so many different ingredients and cultural influences, which have pushed the way I think about food way beyond the northern Italian flavour palate that I grew up with. But on holiday everything is stripped back to a few knives and some pots and pans and whatever I find when I go out each morning – maybe with some money in my hand to meet the fishermen coming off the boats, or at the market to buy fresh local vegetables or rich, creamy burrata. So Puglia, too, has inspired some of the recipes in this book. The ingredients may be more limited, but their quality is exceptional, and that is when I feel at my most creative. I look at what I have and decide then and there how to prepare it for family and friends to share. Just as my grandmother did all those years ago in Corgeno.

I find myself focusing
more and more on
vegetables, not only
for flavour but for
the beauty their
different textures
can bring to a salad
or a dish, sometimes
just by the way
you cut them. I am
excited by the idea of
vegetable butchery.

Seasonal salads and vegetables

Pan-fried cauliflower salad with anchovies and chilli

When I was cooking at the Savoy I thought of myself as the King of the Cauliflower, because one of my jobs was to make the cauliflower soup, and I made a cauliflower cheese that was a work of art, really light and perfectly glazed. But the truth is I never liked cauliflower much. In the cooking of countries like India it is treated to interesting spices, but in European cuisine it often seemed like the boring enemy of gastronomy. In Italy they used to say that cauliflower was for priests, because it kept the sex drive down. But my opinion changed forever a few years ago when I tasted a cauliflower pizza made for me by a husband and wife team, Graham and Kate, when I was a judge at the BBC Radio 4 Food and Farming Awards.

This sweet couple, who now have a restaurant in Bristol, drove around in a bright yellow Defender van with a wood-fired oven called Bertha in the back, and they would come to your party and make maybe 70 or 80 pizzas in a night. Back then it was quite a revolutionary thing to do. I asked them to make me a pizza margherita and another one of their choice. The margherita arrived and it was unbelievably light, Neapolitan style, and I was already thinking, 'These guys are good,' when they brought out their anchovy and cauliflower pizza. Graham had sliced raw cauliflower very thinly and used it instead of cheese. I cannot even describe the way in which it was almost melting and yet it kept its structure and flavour, and its tanginess worked so well with the flavour of the anchovy and a little touch of chilli and lemon zest. It was so delicious and like nothing I had tasted on a pizza before.

When someone presents to you, in such a different way, a vegetable that you have put into a certain compartment of your mind for years and years, it is a total shock. I went back to the kitchen at Locanda and I immediately said to the boys, 'Do we have some cauliflower?' Of course we didn't, because I didn't like it. So I had to go and buy some. We played around with a lot of ideas, and this way of pan-frying the

cauliflower and incorporating it into a salad with anchovies, in a little echo of the pizza flavours, was the one we loved the most. It is exactly the kind of quick and simple salad I like to make if Plaxy and I are at home on our own, or as a starter if friends come around.

When a cauliflower is quite big and loose it is easy to break it into small florets of the same size which will cook evenly, as I suggest here, but if it is smaller and very hard and compact, it can be easier to cut a cross in the base and cook it all in one piece, until just tender. As it cools down, the heat will penetrate evenly all the way through to the centre. Then you can cut it into slices. It's your call, depending on the size and density of the cauliflower.

Or, if you prefer to roast the cauliflower in the oven, you can spread the florets over a baking tray and roast them at 180°C/gas 4 for 20 minutes, sprinkled with a little olive oil. When they have turned golden, remove the tray from the oven and allow them to cool down.

Pan-fried cauliflower salad with anchovies and chilli

1 Rinse the salt from the anchovies and dry them. Run your thumb gently along the backbone of each anchovy – this will allow you to easily pull it out and separate the fish into fillets. **2** Blanch the cauliflower in boiling salted water for 2 minutes. The florets should still be crunchy. Drain them. **3** Heat a little olive oil in a pan, put in the cauliflower and sauté until golden all over. Lift out into a large serving bowl. **4** Add the anchovy fillets, eggs, olives, capers, chilli and parsley. Drizzle in the dressing, mix everything together very gently so that you don't break up the egg yolks any further, and season to taste.

Serves 6

salted anchovies 6

cauliflower 2 heads, separated into florets

olive oil

hard-boiled eggs 3, chopped

black olives 15, stones removed

capers in vinegar 1 tablespoon, drained and rinsed

chopped mild red chilli 1 teaspoon

chopped fresh parsley 1 tablespoon

Giorgio's dressing 200ml (see page 19)

sea salt and freshly ground black pepper

Plaxy's salad

When I first came to London my palate wasn't very spice-oriented. In my region of Lombardy we would occasionally put a little mild chilli into a pasta sauce, but that was it. It was Plaxy who educated me to eat more spicy food, which seemed very daring at the time. But the more you eat, the more you increase your capacity to still taste the flavours of the food and not be distracted by the heat, and so I came to love spice as much as she does.

This has become known as Plaxy's salad because I first made it for her after we had been in Thailand, and she was hankering after the fresh, clean flavours of the food there. I had some carrots and apples, so I put together this very simple combination which has become a favourite at home, and the boys in the kitchen often make big bowlfuls of it when the staff sit down for their meal before the evening service.

It is the combination of fresh carrot, chilli, mint and sweetness that really drives the flavour, so the rest can be quite loose and you can use different fruits if you prefer: perhaps pears or mango. You can leave out the almonds if you like, maybe put in some tomatoes, parsley or coriander, which adds its own radish-ey aroma. Often we grill some chicken breasts and put them on top of the salad and that is lunch, and it is a great salad to put out as part of a barbecue. Of course you can increase or decrease the quantity of chilli, and if you prefer a more citrus dressing, add a little more lemon juice, or if you like a milder flavour, add more olive oil.

Buy fresh, bunched, organic carrots if you can, as you want to get as close as possible to that intense flavour and aroma that a good carrot has when it is just pulled from the ground and that you never forget. When I was small, my grandad had to stop me pulling up all the carrots in the garden, washing them and eating them straight away, like Bugs Bunny. I loved them so much.

Be gentle when you grate the carrots so that you don't bruise them, otherwise they will lose some of their moisture.

Plaxy's Salad

1 Preheat the oven to 180°C/gas 4. **2** Lay the almonds on a baking tray and put them into the oven for about 7 minutes, moving the tray around and giving it a shake occasionally so that the nuts become golden all over. Remove the tray from the oven, allow the nuts to cool then chop roughly. **3** Grate the carrots coarsely into a serving bowl, or, if you want a more beautiful presentation, slice them on a mandoline. **4** Cut the apples in half, take out the core, then slice into segments, leaving the skin on. Add to the carrots, together with the toasted almonds and the mint leaves. **5** In a bowl or jug combine the citrus juice, chilli paste and olive oil, taste and season, then toss this dressing gently through the carrot, apple and almonds and serve straight away.

Serves 6

almonds 250g	
carrots 12	
green apples 3	
fresh mint leaves a good handful	
limes juice of 2, or of 1 lime and 1 lemon	
Thai chilli paste 2 teaspoons, or to taste	
extra virgin olive oil 5 tablespoons	
sea salt and freshly ground black pepper	

Green bean salad with roasted red onions

People often ask how it is possible to get so much flavour into a dish that is essentially green beans and onions in a shallot dressing, but this is a great example of a very simple salad that is all about the quality of the ingredients and the detail of preparing them.

When a green bean is perfectly cooked, if you squeeze and push along the seam with your thumbs it should split easily. Then, a trick I like to do is to run a knife along the length of almost half the beans so that they hold the dressing, along with little slivers of shallot, almond and Parmesan, in a way that a closed bean can't do. The contrast of the closed and open beans creates a slightly different feel in the mouth that makes the salad more interesting.

The real key, though, is the contrasting intense sweetness of the red onions, which comes from roasting them very, very slowly in their skins, but also relies on sweet, fresh onions full of juice to begin with. You can tell easily when you buy them: they shouldn't look dry, and they should feel heavy. The onions we use are the *cipolle di Tropea*, the special Calabrian onions that have their own Protected Geographical Indication label, and are famous for being so sweet you could almost eat them raw. Tropea is on the coast looking out to the Stromboli volcano, and the best onions are grown south of the town and closest to the sea, where the soil is rich with sandy deposits that have blown into it over the 2,000 years since the onions were introduced to Calabria by the Phoenicians. Of course you can use any other variety – the pink French Roscoff are also especially good – but if you can't find really fresh red onions, forget about them; it's better to choose some beautiful sweet, juicy white onions instead.

When onions are slowly roasted like this they can be used for so many other things, too; for example, they are good mixed with roasted vegetables, especially aubergines, or crushed into a paste and served on toasted bread.

The mixing in of the grated Parmesan should be the final touch just before serving, so that it doesn't get soaked into the dressing: that is very important.

I also made this salad for a friend who is vegan, and instead of the Parmesan I pounded a handful of pine kernels with some extra virgin olive oil and just drizzled this over at the end.

Green bean salad with roasted red onions

1 Preheat the oven to 180°C/gas 4. **2** Lay the almonds on a baking tray and put them into the oven for about 7 minutes, moving the tray around and giving it a shake occasionally so that the nuts become golden all over. Remove the tray from the oven, allow the nuts to cool then chop roughly. **3** To roast the red onions, scatter the sea salt over a roasting tray and lay the whole onions on top, still in their skins. Cover with foil and put into the preheated oven for 2 hours. They are ready when they feel quite soft to the touch but still give a little resistance. Take out of the oven and when just cool enough to handle, remove the skin and cut each onion in half. Put into a bowl. **4** Mix together the vinegar, oil and a pinch of salt. Pour over the onions, toss through and leave until completely cool.

5 Blanch the beans in boiling salted water for 4 minutes, depending on their thickness, until they are just tender but retain their bite: they should open out easily if you split them along their length. Then drain them under the cold tap to keep their bright green colour. **6** I like to use the outer layers of onion for decoration. If you want to do this, take off the two outer layers of each onion half, keeping them in one piece, and put to one side. Chop the rest of the onion and mix into the beans, add the shallot dressing and Giorgio's dressing, season and toss all together. **7** Arrange the outer layers of the onions around the outside of a large shallow dish to resemble a crown. Add the grated Parmesan to the bean and onion mixture and turn it all together gently, then spoon it into a mound in the centre of the crown of onions. Sprinkle the almonds on top and finish with some shaved Parmesan.

Serves 6

For the onions:

coarse sea salt 100g, plus an extra pinch

red onions 4 large

red wine vinegar 2 tablespoons

extra virgin olive oil 2 tablespoons

For the beans:

almonds 120g, chopped

long green beans 700g

shallot dressing 3 tablespoons (see page 20)

Giorgio's dressing 100ml (see page 19)

Parmesan 200g, grated, plus a little extra for shaving

Dressings

I am always shocked at how many bottles of dressings and sauces there are in the supermarket, when it is so easy and so much better for you to make your own. Why not invest in some little squeezy bottles to put on that rack on the inside of the door of your fridge, and fill them up with some punchy dressings that you can pull out any time you need something with a kick of flavour to add to a salad, over some vegetables, or a piece of fish or meat. Grate some carrots, add some anchovy dressing from the fridge and you have a starter. The good thing about a squeezy bottle, as opposed to a jar, is that the contents don't come into contact with any utensils, like spoons that have been dipped into other sauces, so the dressings stay pristine. They are all made with oil and vinegar, so they will keep for up to a month, unless you have a son like Jack, in which case it will be a few days.

Giorgio's dressing

This is my everyday dressing. I like a fresh, fruity, grassy, rounded oil, and so just over ten years ago we decided to experiment with producing our own oil in Sicily in partnership with the owner of the small Tenimenti Montoni estate, Antonio Alfano, to use in the restaurant and to sell. The patch of land is high up in the mountains of Cammarata, close to Enna, where they grow Nocellara and Biancolilla olives, and we planted an additional 3,000 olive trees at the top of the mountain which have now come to full production. The oil that they produce is unfiltered, green-gold in colour and full of flavours of tomato and artichoke and cut grass. We have bottles of every single vintage in the kitchen at Locanda, and every autumn when the first new oil comes in it is exciting, because there is always a subtle difference, depending on the season. One year a tempest came in from the sea and did a lot of damage to the trees, but we still managed to produce a beautiful oil. It is such a pleasure and a privilege to open each bottle and to feel that, yes, it has all the rich characteristics of a typical Sicilian oil, but it is also very personal, reflecting all the particularities of a piece of land that you know so well.

1 Put the salt into a bowl. **2** Add the vinegars and leave for a minute to allow the salt to dissolve. **3** Whisk in the olive oil, with 2 tablespoons of water, until the liquids emulsify. Now you can pour the vinaigrette into a clean squeezy bottle and keep it in the fridge for up to a month. It will separate out, so just give it a good shake before you use it.

Makes about 375ml

sea salt ½ teaspoon

red wine vinegar 3 tablespoons

white wine vinegar 2 tablespoons

extra virgin olive oil 300ml, preferably a fruity southern Italian one

Shallot dressing

We use this dressing often for salads, especially when they include roasted onions, sometimes on its own and sometimes combined with Giorgio's dressing on the previous page.

1 Put the shallots into a bowl and season, then add the vinegar.
2 Leave to marinate for 12 hours in the fridge, then pass through a fine sieve and discard the vinegar. Put the onions into a sterilised jar and add the olive oil. You can keep this in the fridge for up to a month.

Makes 150ml

long banana shallots 2, or 4 small round ones, finely chopped
sea salt and freshly ground black pepper
red wine vinegar 75ml
extra virgin olive oil 150ml

Anchovy dressing

Use a blender with a small cup (around 500ml). Blend into a dressing, and store in your squeezy bottle for up to a month.

Makes 200ml

anchovy fillets in oil 14
extra virgin olive oil 120ml
white wine vinegar 3 tablespoons
garlic ½ a clove
dried chilli a pinch (optional)

Sun-dried tomato dressing

Use a blender with a small cup (around 500ml). Blend into a dressing, and store in your squeezy bottle for up to a month.

Makes 200ml

sun-dried tomatoes 8 halves
extra virgin olive oil 100ml
white wine vinegar 2 tablespoons
fresh basil leaves 10
dried oregano a pinch

Black olive dressing

Use a blender with a small cup (around 500ml). Blend into a dressing, and store in your squeezy bottle for up to a month.

Makes 200ml

black olive tapenade 2 tablespoons
anchovy fillets in oil 3
garlic ¼ a clove
extra virgin olive oil 80ml
white wine vinegar 1 tablespoon

Onion and chard salad with broad bean purée

This is a salad that we always made at home, because Margherita could eat everything but the chicory and chilli – although it was a shame she couldn't enjoy them too, because what I love about this is the contrast of the sweetness from the purée, the slight bitterness of the chard, the sweet and sour of the onions, and the chilli. The chilli brings a lift and a liveliness to the salad; it needs to be a detectable flavour, so if you like you can increase the quantity of mild chillies, or use one hotter one instead.

When it first comes into season I like to substitute the Swiss chard with catalogna, one of the members of the big chicory family, which is similar to the Roman puntarelle, except that puntarelle has little spears inside whereas this one is all white-ish-light-green stems and darker green leaves that look a bit like those of a dandelion. In southern Italy catalogna grows wild everywhere, so when you buy your vegetables in the market, the stallholders will often give you a bunch of it as a present, in the way that they might give you a bundle of herbs at other times of the year. People eat it in all sorts of ways, often sautéd with chilli and garlic, or with ricotta. You could also use the blanched version, the Belgian endive, and just cut it into long strips. It will give you the bitterness, but the shapes and texture will be different.

Although you could make the salad with fresh or frozen broad beans (I am always wary of beans in tins, which may have unwanted 'agents' in them), I like to use dried beans. Yes, fresh beans have a fantastic flavour and vivid colour, but dried ones, when they have been soaked and cooked, have a natural viscosity that really helps to bring the purée to the hummus-like consistency that you are looking for. Dried beans are a great gift to humanity: you can keep them in the cupboard or freeze them, you can soak some and if you change your mind about using them straight away you still have 24 hours to use them. And even then, if you cook more than you need, you can cool them down and keep them in a container in the fridge to mix into salads.

When we have the wild fennel, *Finocchio selvatico*, that comes in from Sicily, I like to use it instead of the fennel seeds, or you could use the fronds from a bulb of Florence fennel, chopped very finely and added at the same stage.

I like to serve this with some thick slices of toasted bread so you can mound some of the purée on top then add some of the chard or chicory and onion to get the full experience of sweet, sour, bitter – and a touch of heat.

Onion and chard salad with broad bean purée

1 Soak the beans in cold water overnight. **2** When ready to cook, chop one of the onions and heat 2 tablespoons of olive oil in a large pan. Add the onion and the fennel seeds, or wild fennel or fennel fonds, if using, and cook gently until the onion is soft and translucent. **3** Drain the beans from their soaking water and add to the pan with just enough fresh water to cover. Bring to the boil, then turn down to a simmer for about 1 hour, until tender. Transfer the beans to a blender along with any remaining cooking water (most of it will have been absorbed) and blend, adding 2 more tablespoons of the olive oil, a little at a time, until you have a quite smooth purée that resembles hummus in texture.

4 Chop the rest of the onions. In a separate pan, heat 2 more tablespoons of olive oil, add the onions and cook gently. When soft and translucent, add the vinegar, capers and sugar. Take off the heat, put the lid on the pan and leave to cool down. **5** Cut the stems from the chard or chicory and blanch in boiling salted water for 3 minutes, adding the leaves for 2 more minutes until the stems are tender, then take off the heat and drain. **6** Heat the rest of the olive oil in a large sauté pan, add the garlic and chilli and cook gently for 1 minute. Add the chard or chicory stems and leaves and sauté gently, so they take on the flavours of the garlic and chilli, but don't colour. Season, then take off the heat. **7** Spread the broad bean purée over the base of a serving dish, then layer the chard or chicory and onions on top. Drizzle with extra virgin olive oil and finish with black pepper.

Serves 6

dried broad beans 500g	
white onions 4 medium	
olive oil 150ml	
fennel seeds 1 teaspoon (or 50g wild fennel or fennel fronds, finely chopped)	
white wine vinegar 50ml	
capers in vinegar 2 tablespoons, drained and rinsed	
sugar 1 teaspoon	
Swiss chard or catalogna chicory 2 bunches	
garlic 1 clove, chopped	
mild red chilli 1, chopped	
extra virgin olive oil, to finish	
sea salt and freshly ground black pepper	

Swiss chard with butter, Parmesan and baked eggs

An egg and anything interesting that you have in the fridge is a really good meal. If I am at home by myself I love a fried egg; there is something very comforting about it, cooked slowly in a little bit of salted butter in a non-stick pan, so you really taste the flavour of the eggs – I am not a fan of eggs that have been fried hard and turn brown and crispy around the edges.

Lately I have a penchant for the breakfast made for me by Willie Harcourt-Cooze, who supplies us with his single-estate chocolate: fried egg and smashed avocado on toasted bread, with a little chilli, salt, and some bitter cacao shaved over the top. It has become my favourite thing. And in a way this very straightforward combination of baked egg, Swiss chard and Parmesan touches the same comfort zone. I always think it is a good dish for kids who are not keen on vegetables, because Swiss chard is not known for its huge flavour. It has a sweetness that counteracts the overly bitter edge that other leaves can have, and the umami action of the Parmesan really helps to bring the elements together and makes the combination so delicious – but if you can't find chard, you can substitute fresh, or even frozen, spinach.

100g of Parmesan is great, but if you have 125g that is even better. And if you have an aged Parmesan of 24–36 months, which will have more depth of flavour, that's better still.

1 Preheat the oven to 180°C/gas 4. **2** Cut the stalks from the chard leaves. Blanch the stalks first in boiling salted water for 3 minutes, then add the leaves for a further 2 minutes. Drain, squeezing out the excess water with your hands. **3** Melt the butter in a pan, add the chard, season and toss in the butter briefly, then lift out into an ovenproof dish. Break the eggs on top, season, sprinkle with the Parmesan and put into the preheated oven for about 8–10 minutes, until the whites of the eggs are cooked but the yolks are still soft and the Parmesan is golden. **4** Take out of the oven and serve straight away.

Serves 6

Swiss chard 1.5kg

sea salt and freshly ground black pepper

butter 50g

eggs 6

Parmesan 100g, grated

Aubergines
x 4

I can't think of many ingredients that captivate me in the way that aubergines do. They are so much a part of Italian culture, but over and above the beauty of their many colours – which go from marbled cream and violet to inky purple – I love the aubergine's great capacity to transform itself and agree with flavours and ideas from other cultures. In all the years I have been cooking, the aubergine has surprised me many, many times, and I know that, when I am not expecting it, it will happen again. What is special is that sponginess of texture that you can use to great advantage to absorb other flavours, which, in turn, enhance the slightly bitter flavour of the aubergine, rather than obscuring it.

My first real aubergine revelation, many years ago, was caponata, that Sicilian explosion of sweet and sour vegetables. Then in a fantastic Turkish restaurant in North London, I watched the chef/owner bury a whole aubergine in the ash of a fire pit, so it was protected all around and the skin didn't touch any direct heat. He left it for about 10 minutes then held it upright by its little stalk, peeled it and roughly chopped it with spring onions, seasoned it with lemon juice and salt and pepper and it was so delicious: fresh, yet smoky. I have done the same thing many times since in the summer, burying the aubergines in the ashes of a barbecue. And one of my latest favourite ways to eat aubergine is roasted, covered with miso paste.

It is easy to forget that aubergines have a season, which in the Mediterranean lasts through the summer to autumn. A medium-sized aubergine that is perfectly ripe has a great freshness about it, whereas the older and bigger the fruit, the more bitter it becomes.

To prepare the aubergines for each recipe (apart from the caviar), slice them crossways into 1cm-thick slices. Sprinkle with sea salt and put into a colander to drain for 2 hours to remove some of their bitterness, then rinse and pat dry.

Each recipe overleaf makes enough for 6.

Char-grilled and marinated

This can be a starter or side dish with grilled or roast meat. If you are having a barbecue, you can put the aubergines on the grill first, and have them marinating, while cooking the meat.

1 Prepare 3 aubergines as on the previous page, season with sea salt and freshly ground black pepper, drizzle with olive oil and put on a griddle pan (or barbecue) until the flesh is soft and the skin is marked on both sides (alternatively you can pan-fry them in a non-stick pan with no olive oil over a very low heat until they dry out and become light golden), then lay the slices in a serving dish. **2** With a pestle and mortar, make a marinade by crushing 2 cloves of garlic to a paste, then adding 4 anchovy fillets (drained of their oil) and 20 fresh mint leaves. **3** Continue to pound the ingredients, adding a chopped hot red chilli and 2 pinches of dried oregano, and finally 4 tablespoons of white wine vinegar and 4 tablespoons of extra virgin olive oil. **4** Pour the marinade over the aubergine slices. You can eat them straight away, but they are better kept in the fridge overnight, so that the aubergines really absorb the flavours.

Caviar

This is good as a starter, cooled and spread on bruschetta, or served hot with lamb (you can add some chopped mint at the end).

1 Preheat the oven to 180°C/gas 4. **2** Take 3 large aubergines and cut them in half lengthways, but keep them in pairs. **3** Lay a sprig of rosemary and a slightly crushed clove of garlic over one half of each aubergine. Sprinkle with a little sea salt, then put the halves back together and wrap in foil. **4** Bake in the preheated oven for around 1½ hours, until the aubergines feel soft to the touch. **5** Take out of the oven, discard the rosemary and garlic, scoop out the aubergine flesh and roughly chop it. **6** Heat some olive oil in a large sauté pan, add around 10 finely chopped spring onions and cook them gently until just soft, then add the aubergine and cook until the flesh begins to dry out. **7** Add a tablespoon of tomato purée and cook for another 5 minutes. Taste and season.

Parmigiana

This is a meal in itself, like a lasagne but with aubergine instead of pasta. You need around 1.5 litres of tomato passata and around 300g of Parmesan. Some people like to add mozzarella (you will need 2 x 120g) and chopped cooked ham (around 5 slices), but these are optional.

1 Preheat the oven to 180°C/gas 4. **2** Take about 7 aubergines, prepared as on page 27. Either pan-fry the slices in olive oil (the traditional way) or grill them, brushed with a little oil. If you have fried them, drain them on kitchen paper before assembling. **3** Start by spreading a ladleful of tomato passata thinly over the base of a deep oven dish (this layer should be just enough to coat the aubergine, which goes in next, and not any thicker, or it will make the aubergine too wet). **4** Now put in your layer of aubergine slices, almost overlapping them to avoid any gaps. **5** Sprinkle with plenty of grated Parmesan and a few leaves of basil. If using mozzarella, dot some pieces over the top, and if using cooked ham, scatter in some pieces here, too. **6** Repeat the layers (ideally you should have around 7 layers of aubergine), finishing with plenty of Parmesan. **7** Put into the preheated oven for 30 minutes until golden on top.

Pickled

This will make enough to fill 2 small jars and is a great accompaniment for prosciutto and other antipasti.

1 Prepare 3 aubergines as on page 27, but cut into slices of only around 5mm thick before salting. **2** Slice again into 5mm strips. **3** Bring 300ml of water, 300ml of white wine vinegar and 300ml of white wine to the boil with a teaspoon of sea salt. **4** Put in the aubergine with 2 whole cloves of garlic and cook for 3 minutes, then drain in a colander and pat dry. If you like, you can keep the liquid and store it in the fridge in a plastic container to use next time. **5** Sterilise 2 jars, pack them with the aubergine, garlic and add a sprig of rosemary and a few slices of chilli. **6** Cover with extra virgin olive oil. You can store the jars for a month as long as the aubergine is completely submerged.

Aubergine and sun-dried tomato salad with wild garlic

At one time I used to like to make a carpaccio of aubergines: slicing them very thinly, salting, draining them, rinsing and patting them dry, then grilling them and serving them with chimichurri (see page 227), and at some point that idea developed into this salad. We make it with thicker slices of aubergine, char-grilled and then combined with the sharp kick of spring onions and the sweetness of oven-roasted or sun-dried tomatoes. I like to keep a big bowlful of it in the fridge at home to pull out and have with grilled fish or meat, or just with some toasted bread and maybe some burrata.

1 With a peeler, take off four vertical strips of peel from each aubergine at equal intervals to create a stripy appearance, then slice crossways, 1cm thick. Sprinkle with sea salt and put into a colander to drain for 2 hours, to remove some of the bitterness, then rinse and pat dry.

2 Meanwhile, preheat the oven to 180°C/gas 4. 3 Put the onions, still with their skins on, into a roasting tin, sprinkle with some more sea salt and roast for 2 hours – if you squeeze them gently they should be soft. 4 When cool enough to handle, take off the onion skins and cut the flesh into strips. Sprinkle with the white wine vinegar and a little more sea salt and set aside in a serving dish.

5 Season the slices of aubergine, drizzle with olive oil and cook on a hot griddle pan (or barbecue) until soft and marked on both sides (alternatively, pan-fry them in some olive oil until golden). Allow to cool, then cut into strips of a similar thickness to the onions and mix with the sun-dried or oven-roasted tomatoes in a serving dish. 6 Toss the wild garlic leaves, or parsley and garlic, through the aubergine and onions with the dressing, then taste and season if necessary.

Serves 6
aubergines 3 large
sea salt and freshly ground black pepper
red onions 3
white wine vinegar 1 tablespoon
olive oil
sun-dried or oven-roasted tomatoes 18 (see page 147)
wild garlic leaves 6, when in season, finely chopped (or 1 garlic clove, crushed and then chopped with 1 tablespoon of fresh flat-leaf parsley leaves)
Giorgio's dressing 3 tablespoons (see page 19)

Winter brassica and potato salad

This is the kind of chunky, sturdy winter salad that you can put into the fridge and it will be better the day after you make it. It is good on its own, or to put on the table to extend a family meal. You could use Savoy cabbage, but cavolo nero has a bitterness that really helps. Sometimes I like to add a spoonful of good sauerkraut from a jar on top – the vinegariness and slight spice works really well.

1 Preheat the oven to 180°C/gas 4. **2** To roast the red onions, scatter the sea salt over a roasting tray and lay the whole onions on top, still in their skins. Cover with foil and put into the preheated oven for 2 hours. They are ready when they feel quite soft to the touch but still give a little resistance. Take out of the oven, and when just cool enough to handle remove the skin and cut each onion in half. Put into a bowl. **3** Mix together the vinegar, oil and a pinch of salt. Pour over the onions, toss through and leave until completely cool.

4 Cook the potatoes (skin on) in boiling salted water until tender, then cool, peel and slice. **5** Halve any large florets of romanesco and cauliflower: you want all the pieces to be of a similar size so that they cook consistently. **6** Bring a large pan of salted water to the boil, put in the romanesco for about 3 minutes, depending on the size of the florets, until the pieces are just tender, but still have a little bite, then lift out with a slotted spoon and transfer to a bowl. Repeat with the cauliflower, again cooking for 3 minutes, then the cavolo nero, but cook this for just 1 minute. Finally put in the red cabbage for 4 minutes. When you lift out the red cabbage put it into a separate bowl, or it will stain the other leaves.

7 In a large bowl, crush the potatoes a little and toss with the romanesco, cauliflower, cavolo nero, red onions and 5 tablespoons of the shallot dressing, then season. Transfer to a serving dish. Season the red cabbage and toss with the remaining shallot dressing, then spoon on top of the salad.

Serves 6

coarse sea salt 100g

red onions 4 medium

white wine vinegar 3 tablespoons

extra virgin olive oil
2 tablespoons

sea salt and freshly ground black pepper

potatoes 4 medium

romanesco 1 medium head, separated into florets

cauliflower 1 head, separated into florets

cavolo nero around 300g, spines removed and leaves cut into large pieces

red cabbage 1 small head, sliced

shallot dressing 6 tablespoons (see page 20)

Anchovy and chicory salad with lemon compote

This is one of my favourite salads: it is like a little winter garden of different varieties and colours of chicory all laid down in front of you: green puntarelle, which is the speciality of Rome, round, pink-and-cream-speckled Castelfranco when it comes into season in November, and crimson-and-white-veined radicchio. I like a mix of the long Treviso radicchio which comes from the Veneto, and, in the months between November and March, radicchio tardivo. This is the same variety of chicory, but it has a much more pronounced flavour thanks to an old, ingenious process of cutting and packing the heads of radicchio in baskets in dark forcing sheds with spring water running through. The roots stay immersed in the water and after about ten days, amazing new, crisp, red and white hearts appear and the outer leaves are stripped away.

A winter salad is different to a spring or summer salad: when those delicate, tender leaves are no longer in season what you must have is crunch and character, and I like the bitterness that you get from leaves and vegetables like chicory and artichokes; it is something I have come to enjoy even more as I have got older. We seem to have pulled away from bitterness in our foods, but apart from the extra edge of flavour that it adds, bitter is good for the digestion and helps your liver to function properly.

The green sauce is similar to a classic salsa verde but made without egg or bread, and with some spinach put in with the herbs, and finally there is a little Sicilian soul from the addition of the lemon and chilli compote, which is a bit like a jam with attitude.

It is easy to buy anchovy fillets already marinated in vinegar and oil for this recipe, but try to choose ones in a quite gentle marinade, as some can be too harsh and vinegary. At Locanda we marinate our own fresh anchovies, and it is easy to do if you can find the fresh fish.

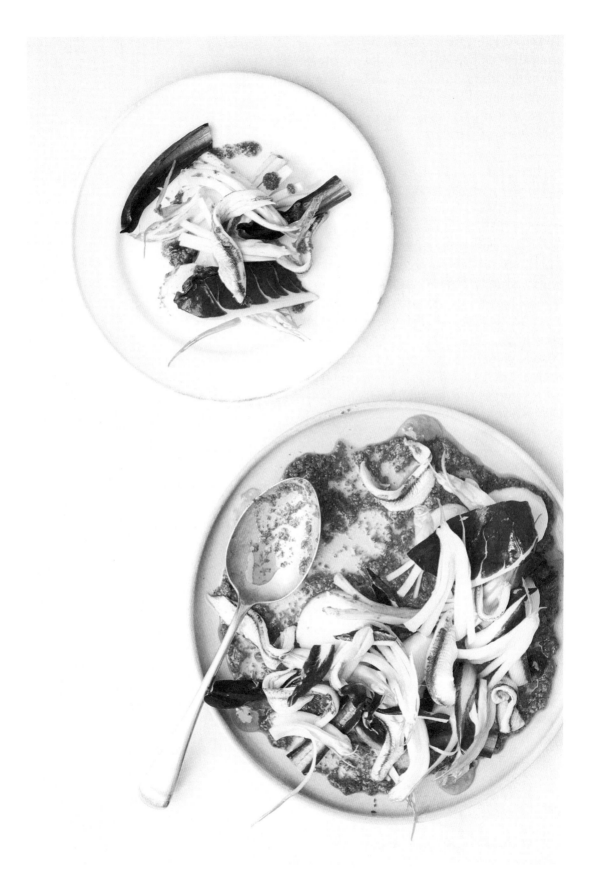

To marinate your own anchovies

You will need around 1kg. Take off the heads, then run your thumbnail along the backbone to remove the fillets and wash them well under running water to remove any traces of blood, which will make the anchovies taste bitter.

Make the marinade by putting 300ml of white wine vinegar and 50g of sea salt into a pan with 500ml of water. Bring to the boil, stirring until the salt has dissolved, then take from the heat and leave to cool down. Put the anchovy fillets into the marinade and leave them in the fridge for 4 hours, moving them around from time to time to make sure they are all completely covered, then lift out and drain in a colander. Put the anchovies into a bowl with 2 chopped cloves of garlic, around 20 large fresh parsley leaves and 10 black peppercorns, then pour in enough extra virgin olive oil to cover. Make sure the anchovies are completely submerged. Once under the oil, the anchovies will keep in the fridge for up to two weeks.

Anchovy and chicory salad with lemon compote (picture on previous page)

1 Preheat the oven to 180°C/gas 4. **2** Scatter a little sea salt over a baking tray, put the potatoes on top and bake in the preheated oven for at least 40 minutes, depending on their size. Remove from the oven and when cool enough to handle, peel and cut into slices about 1cm thick. Put into a bowl, season and toss with half the dressing.

3 Meanwhile, take off the spiky outer leaves of the puntarelle. (Don't throw them away, as you can blanch them and sauté them in olive oil, with a little garlic and chilli, as an accompaniment to meat or fish, or use them in the salad on page 77.) Now you will see at the base of the puntarelle the fat, hollow, spear-like stems that are white at the bottom, turning green, and have tendrils growing out from them. Cut these free, then, with a small knife, make vertical cuts all around the base of the stems, put them into a colander and drain under cold running water for 5 minutes, to remove some of the bitterness. Then transfer them to a bowl of iced water for about an hour and you will see that the cuts in the stems will allow them to twist and curl like little flowers in the icy cold.

4 To make the lemon compote, remove the peel from the lemons using a sharp knife, and discard it. Then separate into segments,

Serves 6

sea salt

potatoes 4 large, skin on, washed

Giorgio's dressing 200ml
(see page 19)

puntarelle 1 small head

radicchio di Treviso 1

radicchio di Castelfranco 1

radicchio tardivo 1

marinated anchovy fillets about 500g (or about 10 per person)

For the lemon compote:

lemons 10

caster sugar 200g

mild red chilli ½

For the green sauce:

spinach leaves 80g

salted anchovies 6

garlic 1 clove, peeled

fresh flat-leaf parsley 100g

white wine vinegar 1 tablespoon

extra virgin olive oil 200ml

removing the skin, and put into a pan. Squeeze the rest of each lemon over the top, so that any additional juice goes into the pan. Add the sugar and chilli to the pan, slowly bring to a simmer and cook gently for 10 minutes until you have a pale syrup. Take off the heat, put the contents of the pan into a blender and blend until smooth, then keep to one side.

5 You can make the green sauce using either a pestle and mortar or a blender. First, blanch the spinach very briefly in boiling salted water – just lower it in and then lift it out again – then drain it in a colander under cold running water, to stop it from cooking any further and keep it looking fresh and green. **6** Rinse the salt from the 6 salted anchovies and dry them. Run your thumb gently along the backbone of each one, which will allow you to easily peel it out and separate the fish into fillets, then just roughly chop them. **7** If using a pestle and mortar, crush the garlic first, then add the anchovies and continue to crush. Add the parsley leaves and keep on working the ingredients into a paste. Add the spinach and work it in. Finally, mix in the vinegar and oil. You should finish up with a smooth bright green paste. If using a blender, you can put all the ingredients in together and blend as quickly as possible, to a smooth paste.

8 Cut the base from the heads of radicchio to release the leaves and wash them under running water. Pat dry and put into a bowl. Drain the puntarelle 'flowers' from their iced water and pat them dry too, then add them to the bowl and toss with the rest of the dressing. **9** To assemble the salad, spread the green sauce over the base of a large serving dish and arrange the potato slices on top. Drain the marinated anchovies, then intersperse them with the dressed leaves and puntarelle 'flowers'. Dot teaspoonfuls of lemon compote onto some of the leaves and serve.

Courgettes
x 4

My grandad used to grow courgettes in the garden and I remember when I was small thinking, 'These plants take up such a massive space, and all you get is about three courgettes,' so the first time I saw a whole boxful I thought it must take miles and miles of garden to grow them. I believe that to produce a good courgette the plant must have its roots in the ground, and preferably be grown organically, which seems to make a massive difference to the taste and smell, rather than using the hydroponic culture, which I feel produces a more watery courgette. I visited an amazing farm in the desert in Dubai, where an incredible woman, Elena Kinane, was growing organic courgettes, as well as around 120 different heirloom varieties of fruit, vegetables and herbs, in a tiny, shadowy area of sand in a valley between some massive dunes. One of the crops she grew was alfalfa, which went to feed local racing camels, then the manure from the animals was sent back to fertilise the sand. It was such an extraordinary thing to suddenly come across this green oasis in such a harsh environment. She had an irrigation system, and glasshouses, more to keep the produce cool than hot, and every so often an amazing storm of coldish wet air would be created inside. The courgettes were her obsession, and the whole operation was so inspirational, it gave me hope that there are always people with the will and the ingenuity to produce food and survive in the harshest of environments.

There is a certain sweetness and particularity of flavour about courgettes that kids seem to like, in the same way as peas. We always had them at home for Margherita because although she was allergic to so many green vegetables, she could eat courgettes, and she loved them. I only wish we saw more interesting varieties, as so many seem to have disappeared in favour of the universal sleek green one. Where are the yellow ones, the ones that are so pale green they are almost white, and the round ones that are the perfect shape for stuffing?

Each recipe makes enough for 6.

Marinated

You can eat the courgettes on their own, in a salad, or serve them with burrata, or fish.

1 Cut 6 large courgettes lengthways into thin slices (about 3mm) with a sharp knife or mandoline. Heat some olive oil in a sauté pan and fry the courgettes until golden on each side. Lift out and drain on kitchen paper. **2** Very finely chop a handful of large fresh mint leaves with a small handful of fresh parsley leaves and 2 cloves of garlic, and mix with about a teaspoon of dried chilli. **3** In a large pan heat 500ml of extra virgin olive oil to 120°C (just under a simmer). Very slowly and carefully add 70ml of white wine vinegar and allow to bubble up for a minute. Take off the heat and leave to cool. **4** Layer some of the courgettes in a serving dish, sprinkle with some of the herb and garlic mixture, then spoon in some of the oil and vinegar. Repeat until you have used up all the components. Cover with clingfilm and leave in the fridge to marinate for 24 hours.

Pan-fried with garlic, tomato and white wine

This is a good side dish for white meat, fish, or whatever you like.

1 Put a clove of garlic on a chopping board, and with the back of a large knife, crush it into a paste. **2** Put a large handful of fresh parsley leaves on top and chop finely, so that the garlic and parsley combine and release their flavours into each other. **3** Cut 3 medium courgettes in half lengthways, then slice into half-moons about 5mm thick. Heat some olive oil in a large sauté pan, add 2 lightly crushed cloves of garlic and cook gently until golden (take care not to let them burn). Add the courgettes, season with sea salt and freshly ground black pepper, then spread them out so that they are all in contact with the pan and sauté quickly – you will need to do this in batches – until golden on both sides. **4** Add half a glass (35ml) of white wine and about 5 halved cherry tomatoes to the pan and cook for about 3 minutes. Remove the whole garlic cloves and sprinkle in the parsley and garlic mixture.

Deep-fried

1 With a mandoline, cut about 3 large courgettes into long, thin strips. The trick is to cut only two strips from each side: one, two, then turn, one, two, turn, so you get a homogenous amount of firm white courgette and courgette with a little bit of skin attached. That way when you fry them they will be fantastically crispy, whereas if you carry on cutting all the way through to the soft middle of the courgette when you fry those strips they will just turn to mush. **2** Put the strips into a shallow bowl, season with sea salt and leave for about 30 minutes, until some of the water has been drawn out. **3** Mix equal quantities of 00 flour and semolina flour in a shallow bowl and lift the courgettes into the flour. Don't rinse, drain or squeeze them, as you want them to be moist, so that the flour will cling to them. **4** Heat some vegetable oil to 180°C in a deep-fryer (alternatively, heat the oil in a large pan, no more than a third full – if you don't have a kitchen thermometer, drop a little flour into the oil and it will sizzle very gently). **5** Lower the floured courgettes into the hot oil and fry for a few minutes until golden and crisp. **6** Drain on kitchen paper and sprinkle with sea salt to taste.

Stuffed

For a starter or a light lunch, you need 8 courgettes.

1 Cut 6 of the courgettes lengthways and scoop out the seeds. Sprinkle with sea salt and put into a colander for an hour to draw out some of the water and season the courgettes at the same time. Rinse and pat dry. **2** Meanwhile, heat some olive oil in a pan, add a diced onion and 2 diced stalks of celery, and cook gently until the onion is soft and translucent. **3** Add 2 tablespoons of white wine vinegar, bring to the boil, stir in a tablespoon of tomato passata and take off the heat. **4** Preheat the oven to 180°C/gas 4 and line a roasting tin with baking paper. Chop the remaining 2 courgettes and an aubergine. **5** Heat some olive oil in a sauté pan and fry both together until golden. Add to the onion and tomato mixture, stirring in a little extra tomato passata if the mixture is too dry. **6** Spoon into the cavities of the courgettes and lay them in the lined roasting tin. Put into the preheated oven and bake for about 20 minutes, until the vegetable stuffing has turned dark golden.

Creamed salt cod salad with cicerchia purée

Salt cod has become very fashionable, and yet the technique of salting and then drying fish goes back hundreds of years. It is hard for us to understand now how important and valuable salt cod was to inland regions of Italy and other Mediterranean countries in the days before refrigeration, especially on Fridays, the traditional fish day decreed by the Catholic church. In some remote areas, where animals couldn't easily graze, salt cod possibly even kept some families alive. Take a region like Calabria, which has a big beautiful coast full of lovely fish, but the mountains are so close to the sea that only a short distance away the only fish that would have been available would be salted and dried. There is a particular village, Gerace, which was known for its salt cod, because the people used to soak it in the local spring, and there is still a shop there where you can buy the whole salted fish, which look like prehistoric creatures.

I remember, also, that my grandmother thought that the fish would be better if you soaked it under the fountain in our village of Corgeno. She used to de-salt it and cook fat pieces of it in milk, with onions and garlic, *alla vicentina*, in the style of the town of Vicenza in the north of Italy, or *in umido*, with tomatoes and onions, but my favourite is to turn it into a creamy paste, as in this recipe and the one that follows. It is quite magical to see the transformation of this fibrous fish as you beat it, adding olive oil very, very gently until it becomes whiter and whiter. You do need to use a lighter northern oil, such as a Ligurian one, though, as a strong green Sicilian or Tuscan oil will give a green tinge to the cod, and also impose its own flavour too much.

With the popularity of salt cod, it is now easy to buy it already de-salted. In the markets in Italy, there will often be a salt cod specialist selling it both ways, in many different cuts. There may be a few eggs or anchovies on the stall, but nothing else. It is all about the salt cod. But if you are soaking it yourself, you need to do this in cold water in the fridge, for up to three days, changing the water every day, depending on the thickness and the particular cut of cod.

The creamed cod is fantastic just on its own with a little salad as a starter, and it makes a great crostini to put out with drinks. You can have it ready in a bowl in the fridge and toast your bread in advance and keep it in an airtight container. Then you can just scoop some of the creamed cod on to the pieces of toast and put some halved cherry tomatoes on top, if you like. I was once served creamed salt cod on top of a thick, firm slice of a green Cuore di Bue – the massive, ribbed ox-heart tomato – which had been pan-fried really quickly, and it was fantastic.

Cicerchia is an ancient chickpea-like legume (known in Britain as the grass pea) that is one of the almost-extinct crops that has been revived and championed and made fashionable by the Slow Food movement. It used to be grown as a peasant crop in many countries, including Italy, because it can grow in areas where conditions are harsh, and so in times of famine it was very important. Then it fell out of favour, after it was discovered that it contained a neurotoxin called diaminopropionic acid, and if it was eaten as a major part of the diet over a period of time (as could happen during times of famine) it could cause paralysis of the lower limbs in adults and brain damage in children. However, in small quantities it is now known to be harmless. In fact it is considered to be nutritious, as well as full of flavour – but if you prefer, you can use chickpeas. If you can find good chickpeas in jars, that have no thickeners or other unwanted ingredients added, and not too much salt, you can use them instead.

Creamed salt cod salad with cicerchia purée

1 Soak the cicerchia (or dried chickpeas, if using) and the beans in separate bowls of water overnight. **2** Preheat the oven to 180°C/gas 4. **3** Mix the shallots, capers and anchovies in a bowl. **4** Lay the cod in a deep roasting tray and spread the shallot, caper and anchovy mixture over the top. Add 3 of the garlic cloves and 4 of the bay leaves and pour the milk over the top, then cover with foil. Bake in the preheated oven for 2½–3 hours, until the cod breaks into soft flakes, then remove and keep to one side. Turn the oven down to 150°C/gas 2. **5** Line a baking tray with baking paper and lay the slices of pancetta on top. Put into the oven for 40 minutes, until crispy, then lift out.

6 Meanwhile, drain the cicerchia or chickpeas and beans, discarding the water. Rinse under running water and put into separate pans with enough fresh water to cover. Add another clove of garlic, a bay leaf, and a few sage leaves to each pan. Bring to the boil, then turn down to a simmer and cook until tender (each one will take roughly an hour). Take off the heat, leave to cool down in the cooking water, then drain. Keep back half the cicerchia or chickpeas then mix the rest with the beans in a bowl. If using jarred or tinned chickpeas, add half now, but keep the rest, with their liquid. **7** Heat a frying pan, add the diced pancetta and sauté until crisp and golden. Lift out and drain on kitchen paper, then add to the bowl, together with the lamb's lettuce. **8** Take the reserved cicerchia or chickpeas and put into a blender, adding 3 tablespoons of the olive oil a little at a time, until you have a creamy purée. If using jarred or tinned chickpeas, heat them up with enough of their liquid to cover before blending. Keep to one side.

9 Put the remaining garlic cloves on a chopping board and with the back of a large knife, crush them into a paste. Put the parsley leaves on top and chop finely, so that the garlic and parsley combine and release their flavours into each other. **10** Lift the cod from the cooking milk and put it into the bowl of a food mixer. Pour the milk and the shallot, caper and anchovy mixture through a fine sieve, discarding the milk. Add the drained anchovy mixture to the cod and mix slowly, adding the rest of the olive oil a little at a time, to avoid splitting the mixture, until you have a creamy consistency. Towards the end of mixing, add the chopped parsley and garlic. **11** To serve, spread the cicerchia or chickpea purée over the base of a shallow serving dish. Toss the rest of the cicerchia or chickpeas and beans with the lamb's lettuce and dressing and scatter over the purée. Spoon the creamed salt cod over the top and finish with the crispy slices of pancetta.

Serves 6

dried cicerchia, or chickpeas 300g, or the equivalent good jarred or tinned ones

dried cannellini or other white beans 150g

dried borlotti beans 150g

shallots 100g, finely chopped

salted capers 40g, rinsed

anchovy fillets in oil 12, rinsed

de-salted salt cod 1kg

garlic 8 cloves, whole

bay leaves 7

milk 2 litres

pancetta 6 thin slices

fresh sage leaves a small bunch

diced pancetta 200g

lamb's lettuce 300g

delicate extra virgin olive oil, for example Ligurian 300ml

fresh flat-leaf parsley a handful

Giorgio's dressing 150ml (see page 19)

Creamed salt cod salad with confit cherry tomatoes

This is a variation on the previous recipe to make in summer when you have good, ripe cherry tomatoes. The salt cod has a very deep, rich flavour, and the acidity of the tomatoes and the pepperiness of the watercress offset it perfectly. I really like it with crunchy polenta crisps (see page 263).

1 If you are making the polenta crisps, these need to be started off the night before. **2** Preheat the oven to 180°C/gas 4. **3** Mix the shallots, capers and anchovies in a bowl. **4** Lay the cod in a deep roasting tray and spread the shallot, caper and anchovy mixture over the top. Add 3 of the garlic cloves and 4 of the bay leaves and pour the milk over the top, then cover with foil. Bake in the preheated oven for 2½–3 hours, until you can break the cod easily into soft flakes. Keep to one side. **5** Meanwhile, lay the tomatoes in a single layer in a shallow heatproof dish. Heat half the olive oil very gently in a pan with a garlic clove, bay leaf and rosemary – just until the odd bubble breaks the surface and the herbs begin to lightly fry (around 70–80°C if you have a thermometer). Take off the heat and pour over the tomatoes, so that they are completely covered. Leave for 2 hours, until cool.

6 Put the remaining garlic cloves on a chopping board, and with the back of a large knife, crush them into a paste. Put the parsley leaves on top and chop finely, so that the garlic and parsley combine and release their flavours into each other. **7** Lift the cod from the cooking milk and put it into the bowl of a food mixer. Pour the milk and anchovy mixture through a fine sieve, discarding the milk. Add the drained anchovy mixture to the cod and mix slowly, adding the rest of the olive oil a little at a time, to avoid splitting the mixture, until you have a creamy consistency. Towards the end of mixing, add the parsley and garlic. **8** Drain the tomatoes, but retain the oil. Halve the tomatoes and put into a serving dish. Add the watercress, season and dress with about 3 tablespoons of the oil reserved from marinating the tomatoes, together with the white wine vinegar. Serve with the creamed salt cod and the polenta crisps, if you like.

Serves 6

shallots 100g, finely chopped
salted capers 40g, rinsed
anchovy fillets in oil 12, rinsed
de-salted salt cod 1kg
garlic 6 cloves, whole
bay leaves 5
milk 2 litres
cherry tomatoes 1kg
olive oil 500ml
fresh rosemary 1 sprig
fresh flat-leaf parsley a handful
watercress leaves 2 bunches
sea salt and freshly ground black pepper
white wine vinegar 1 tablespoon

To serve:
polenta crisps (see page 263), (optional)

Cappon magro

I love this. I know the recipe looks a little long and scary, but it's such a beautiful thing to do if you have lots of friends coming around in the summer, so I just had to include it. It is a huge celebratory feast of fish and vegetables from Genoa, the capital of Liguria, which is a region that is such a tight fit in between the sea and the mountains, and this is an incredible marriage of the bounty of both. I have never found the idea of surf and turf acceptable in the form of steak with lobster – for me these are two things that should not be put together – whereas the combination of seafood and hearty vegetables works so well, especially as each ingredient stays recognisable in its texture and taste within the structure of the dish, which layers its way up from quite rich and saucy at the base, to the delicate ingredients on top.

Like so many dishes that ended up as elaborate baroque centrepieces on rich men's tables, *cappon magro* has its roots in the meals that fishermen ate at sea, made with galettes – hard biscuits – which would be soaked in sea water to soften them and then layered up with some of the fish they caught and boiled up, along with root vegetables which would either have been stored on board or preserved in vinegar – the genesis of the vinegary salsa verde (green sauce) that binds the layers together. I have given a recipe for the galettes (once made you can store them in an airtight container for a few weeks), but you could use water biscuits instead.

Cappon magro was one of the dishes that the great Italian chef Nino Bergese was most proud to put his name to. He was one hell of a guy, who cooked for royalty and film stars and was the first chef to earn two Michelin stars at his restaurant, La Santa, in Genoa, but he never forgot the traditional dishes of his region. The way I do the dish is a little different, because I like to add hake. Sometimes we make it at Locanda, where the challenge is to incorporate all the ingredients into individual plates, but personally I like to make one big dish of it, as it looks so splendid. This is the kind of thing I would do when I am relaxed on holiday with family and friends and can buy a box

of mixed fish and shellfish and really fresh vegetables in the market. The nature of it is that you can adjust the ingredients according to what you can find, so if you have to leave out the artichoke or beetroot, depending on the season, it really doesn't matter; if you can't find hake, another white fish will be fine, and you can leave out the bottarga, too, if you prefer.

Cappon magro

1 Preheat the oven to 180°C/gas 4. **2** To make the galettes, mix all the ingredients together in a large bowl until you have a firm ball of dough. Leave to rest for 20 minutes, covered with a clean tea towel, then roll out thinly (2–3mm) and prick with a fork. With a 4cm diameter cutter, cut out discs (you should get around 25–30). Lift on to a baking tray, or trays, and put into the preheated oven to bake for about 10 minutes, until light golden. Remove and keep to one side.

3 Cook the potatoes and Jerusalem artichokes, whole, in a large pan of boiling salted water until tender. **4** Meanwhile, cook the whole carrots, celery and beans, in a separate pan of boiling salted water, lifting out each vegetable as soon as it is tender, and draining under cold running water. Finally put the beetroot into the same pan of boiling salted water (don't add it until all the other vegetables are out, as it will stain them red) and cook until soft, then drain and set aside with the rest of the cooked vegetables.

5 Bring a fresh pan of salted water to the boil with the halved lemon and peppercorns, and put in the lobster tails, if using, and cook for 4 minutes. Alternatively, if using prawns, cook with the langoustines, for just one minute then remove. Then put in the mussels and cook until they open (remove any that don't). Lift out, then put in the clams and cook until they open (again, remove any that don't). Lift out, then finally put in the hake and cook until tender. Lift out and keep to one side.

6 Now you need to make the green sauce. Rinse the salt from the anchovies and dry them. Run your thumb gently along the backbone of each anchovy – this will allow you to easily pull it out and separate the fish into fillets. Heat a little olive oil in a pan, add the fennel and cook briefly until just soft. Lift out and allow to cool, then put into a blender with the rest of the ingredients and 550ml warm water and blend into a green sauce. **7** Cut all the reserved cooked vegetables into slices and put them into separate bowls, then season each one with a tablespoon of Giorgio's dressing and some salt and pepper.

8 Take the skin from the hake and flake the fish. Put into a separate bowl with half the white wine vinegar and the olive oil. **9** Take the shells from the lobster tails or prawns (if using prawns, leave the heads on). Take half the mussels and clams out of their shells (reserving the rest for garnish). **10** Put the rest of the white wine vinegar into a large shallow bowl with 125ml water and put the galettes into the bowl to soak for a few minutes.

Serves 10

potatoes 4 medium
Jerusalem artichokes 3
sea salt and freshly ground black pepper
carrots 4 large, peeled
celery 4 stalks
green beans 200g
red beetroot 2 large
lemon 1, halved
black peppercorns a few
lobster tails 3, and/or 20 large prawns in their shells
langoustines 12
mussels 15, cleaned and prepared as on page 100
clams 1kg, cleaned and prepared as on page 100
hake fillets 800g
Giorgio's dressing 6 tablespoons (see page 19)
white wine vinegar 150ml
extra virgin olive oil 50ml
oysters 6, shells washed and opened
pickled artichokes 4 (see page 76)
hard-boiled eggs 3, quartered
pea shoots 500g (optional)
bottarga 1 slice of

For the galettes:
00 flour 300g
semolina flour 200g
polenta flour 50g
fine table salt 15g
fresh yeast 15g
extra virgin olive oil 100ml

For the green sauce:
salted anchovies 3
olive oil
fennel 70g, chopped
capers in vinegar 1 tablespoon
hard-boiled egg 1
breadcrumbs, made from stale bread 1 tablespoon
white wine vinegar 60ml
black olives 20g, stones removed
garlic 1 small clove
extra virgin olive oil 80ml
cold water 20ml

11 To assemble the salad the idea is to layer up the hake, galettes and sauce with a different vegetable each time, starting and finishing with the sauce. So you will need seven layers of the sauce, and five layers each of the flaked hake and galettes.

12 First, spread a fifth of the green sauce over the base of a large serving dish, then spread a fifth of the hake over the top, followed by all of the carrots in an even layer, then a fifth of the whole soaked galettes, spread out evenly. Next, spread over another fifth of the sauce, followed by another fifth of the hake, all the celery and another fifth of the galettes. Repeat, this time with the potatoes, then again with the Jerusalem artichokes, and the beetroot, and finishing with a layer of galettes and another layer of sauce. Garnish the top as decoratively as you like, with the lobster tails and/or prawns, langoustines, mussels, clams, the oysters in their shells, pickled artichokes, hard-boiled eggs, green beans, pea shoots if using, and shavings of bottarga.

Giardiniera (pickled vegetables)

When I was growing up in Italy it was part of the fabric of life to grow your own vegetables or buy them in the market when they were in season, and at their most prolific, then prepare some to keep under oil or pickle them in vinegar in jars for the rest of the year, ready to put out with some prosciutto or salami if someone special called around. It is a tradition Plaxy and I always carried on when the kids were younger, because I liked the idea that anyone could come home at any time, especially after a journey, and there would be some *carta di musica* (see page 126) in the cupboard, some cured meats in the fridge, and jars of vegetables as in this recipe, or onions, as in the recipe that follows, to put out with them.

Our village, Corgeno, only had one butcher, Stefanino, and they would kill a cow once a week, outside. My brother and I would be coming home from school, and we would stop and wait to see the guys kill the cow under the supervision of the vet before we went home, which was an important thing, because it taught us where our food came from, and to respect the animals that were providing it. Every part of the animal needed to be sold: the tripe, lungs, heart and the bones for the dogs. Stefanino knew everybody in the village and who liked what, and he would say to my mother sometimes, 'I kept you the knees' – clearly the animal only had four legs, so I am sure he had to rotate these specialities between people. My mother would simmer these pieces of bone very slowly – I can still smell it now. Then she would pull off all the bits of meat and cartilage, chop them up and mix them with the giardiniera, to make *insalata di nervetti*. I used to hate it at the time, but now I love it: all the different consistencies of soft and gristly meat mixed with the sweet-and-sourness of the peppers, carrots, cauliflower and courgettes: so delicious.

1 In a pan mix the olive oil, vinegar, sugar and salt and stir to dissolve the sugar. Add the chopped vegetables and chilli and bring to the boil, stirring regularly, then immediately take off the heat and leave the vegetables to cool down in the liquid. **2** Once cold, store in sterilised jars in the fridge for up to a month.

Makes several jars

extra virgin olive oil 1.5 litres	
red wine vinegar 1.5 litres	
caster sugar 300g	
sea salt 150g	
cauliflowers 3, separated into small florets	
red peppers 3, deseeded and cut into squares about 1cm	
yellow peppers 3, deseeded and cut into squares about 1cm	
carrots 6 large, cut into cubes about 1cm	
courgettes 6 large, cut into cubes about 1cm	
red onions 3, sliced vertically	
white onions 3, sliced vertically	
mild red chillies 6 large, chopped	

Sweet and sour baby onions

1 In a pan mix the olive oil, vinegars, sugar and salt and stir to dissolve the sugar. Add the onions and bring to the boil, stirring regularly, then immediately take off the heat and leave the onions to cool down in the liquid. **2** Once cold, store in a sterilised jar in the fridge for up to a month.

Makes 1 large jar

extra virgin olive oil 750ml	
red wine vinegar 750ml	
balsamic vinegar 350ml	
caster sugar 150g	
sea salt 75g	
baby onions 2kg, peeled	

Pinzimonio

I can tell a lot about someone by the way they prepare their *pinzimonio*, which is nothing more complicated than raw vegetables cut up and put out with a sauce (typically *bagna cauda*, made with anchovies and garlic) to dip into as an aperitivo before lunch or dinner.

In the 70s and 80s the fashion was to cut vegetables into identical short, sharp, geometrical shapes, then slowly, slowly they began to appear more loosely, until the 90s, when everyone began to acknowledge that vegetables should just look natural. Personally I have always thought that when you slice vegetables for *pinzimonio*, you should follow their shape and structure as much as possible.

You can add or subtract any vegetable you like, and instead of the sauces suggested here you can put out anything you want, maybe some olive or sun-dried tomato paste loosened with extra virgin olive oil, or even a spicy chimichurri (see page 227), made with plenty of very finely chopped parsley (and/or coriander), oregano, garlic, shallots and chilli, seasoned and mixed with some olive oil, vinegar and lemon juice.

(see picture on previous page)

1 Cut all the vegetables into thin strips lengthways and lay them on a bed of crushed ice to keep them crisp. Put into the fridge while you make the sauces.

2 For the *bagna cauda*, put the milk and garlic into a small pan and bring to the boil, then turn down the heat and simmer for about 20 minutes, until the garlic is soft. Just before you take it off the heat, put the anchovies into a shallow heatproof bowl with a little olive oil and the knob of butter and place it over the pan, for a minute or two, until the anchovies 'melt'. Take the pan off the heat and press the anchovy mixture through a fine sieve into a bowl. Crush the garlic with a little of the milk in which it was cooked and stir into the anchovy mixture. Loosen if necessary with a little more olive oil.

3 For the artichoke sauce, prepare the artichokes as on page 63, and cut into quarters. **4** Heat a little olive oil in a pan, add the onion and cook gently until soft and translucent, add the artichokes, wine and lemon juice and bring to the boil, then add the vegetable stock and bay leaf and cook for about 10 minutes, until the artichokes are soft. **5** Lift out the artichokes and put into a blender with half the cooking liquid. Blend to a purée, adding more of the cooking liquid if necessary. Taste and season as necessary, adding a little more lemon juice if it isn't sharp enough. Drizzle with a little extra virgin olive oil and put out alongside the *bagna cauda*. **6** To serve, I like to put some more crushed ice in the base of a large deep glass bowl, and put in the raw vegetable strips so that they are standing upright, and everyone can take pieces as they like and dip them into the sauces.

Serves 6

carrots 2
celery 3 stalks
cucumber 1
fennel 1 bulb
radicchio tardivo 1
yellow pepper 1
red pepper 1
asparagus 1 small bunch when in season
radishes 1 bunch

For the bagna cauda:
milk 9 tablespoons
garlic 9 cloves
anchovies in oil 12, drained
extra virgin olive oil a little
butter a knob

For the artichoke sauce:
artichokes 5
olive oil a little
onion 1, finely chopped
white wine ½ glass (35ml)
lemon juice of 1
good vegetable stock 150ml
bay leaf 1
sea salt and freshly ground black pepper

Vignarola (braised spring vegetables)

Simple springtime vegetable dishes like this have always figured highly in our family. When we were on holiday in Sicily, I used to make a little stew that Margherita could have, with the long, bendy, green *zucca trombetta*, which is a kind of cross between a courgette and a pumpkin. I would sauté it with onions and garlic, add some spinach and peas, cover it with white wine and simmer it for 20 minutes or so.

Vignarola is simply a celebration of that moment in spring when you have an abundance of beautiful artichokes, and the first of the broad beans and peas. In the restaurants in Rome they will bring out little dishes of bright green vignarola along with artichokes *alla Romana* (see page 64) and *fritti* (see page 65), with baskets of bread and olive oil, and sometimes bowls of the first young broad beans of the season. You open up the pods and there are maybe only three or four tiny beans inside, which you eat raw with pieces of pecorino and pepper. Such a wonderful collection of flavours and textures.

Vignarola is so simple, but what makes it special is that the vegetables are cooked one after the other in olive oil and with the tiniest amount of water, so that each one tastes totally of itself. As the season goes on you can take some vegetables away and add others, such as spinach or chard, but keep the essence of the dish by using good frozen broad beans and peas. I like to have any that is left over in the fridge to smash up for a sandwich, to put out with burrata and toasted bread, or warm up alongside some grilled chicken or steak. One morning when Plaxy and I were on holiday in Puglia in the spring, for brunch I made a vignarola quickly with fresh peas and beans I had bought in the market along with some *cime di rapa* (turnip tops). I toasted some bread, fried a couple of local farm eggs, broke them up and mixed them into the vegetables, which I crushed a little bit, and we ate from bowls, sitting looking out at the sea, and it felt like some of the best food I had made in my life.

1 Prepare the artichokes as on page 63 and cut into quarters. **2** Heat a little olive oil in a pan, add the spring onions and cook briefly. **3** Drain the artichokes and add to the pan. Season, cover and cook for 2 minutes. **4** Add the broad beans with a couple of tablespoons of water and cook for another 2 minutes, then add the peas, plus another 2 tablespoons of water. Cook for another 2 minutes, adding a little more water if necessary. Each vegetable should now be tender and the water should have been absorbed. **5** Finish with the mint leaves. Eat warm or cold.

Serves 6

artichokes	4 small
olive oil	a little
spring onions	5, chopped
sea salt and freshly ground black pepper	
podded fresh broad beans	200g
podded fresh peas	200g
fresh mint leaves	10

Artichokes
x 4

I know I cannot claim artichokes (*carciofi*) only for Italy, but they are such a quintessential ingredient, so steeped in Italian history, and things of such beauty and fascination that they have been captured many times in Italian art. There is even a famous Italian bitter liqueur, invented in the 1950s, called Cynar, from *Cynara scolymus*, the botanical name for artichoke. It is made with various plants and herbs, but artichokes are the main flavouring and the dark bottle has an iconic bright red label with a green artichoke on it. Usually you drink it as a *spritzino*, mixed with prosecco and soda water. I remember when I was quite young seeing an advert on TV set in a square outside a bar in Milan where fashionable people sat around tables drinking Cynar underneath a massive metal sculpture of an artichoke.

There is another story that the name Cynar comes from Greek mythology: Zeus, the ruler of the sky and all the gods, was besotted with the nymph Cynara, who drove him mad with jealousy, so he transformed her into a spiky artichoke to remind him of both the green of her eyes and the pain she caused him.

Artichokes were developed by the Arabs in Sicily and first found their way onto the mainland in the sixteenth century, when the Jewish people were expelled during the Spanish Inquisition and artichokes were one of the ingredients they took with them. The first artichokes were said to be very hard, even more spiny and very bitter, but over the years they have been cultivated to be sweeter, softer and more friendly, though they retain that very special tinny flavour that I love, either when they are raw, or when simply boiled whole with a little bit of butter.

The artichokes that I like most are the small spiny ones, which have a deep, essential, slightly bitter flavour, but small doesn't necessary equal tender. Even bigger artichokes can be tender. What is important is not size, but age. The fresher the better: look at the stem of the artichoke and it should be green, not turning black.

Artichokes
x 4

Artichokes in cooking

Artichokes are fantastic on their own, but their elegant touch of bitterness gives so much depth of flavour to other dishes. An artichoke risotto is beautiful, and if I make a vegetable lasagne, I always want to put artichoke in there, as it goes so well with the béchamel and cheese, and adds its own texture to that of the other vegetables.

When we used to go on holiday every summer in Sicily, artichokes were one of my favourite things to put into a frittata, or to make into a little stew like vignarola (see page 58) with other spring vegetables, or to mix with other greens in the chicory family, maybe with some potatoes added, to serve with some chicken or a pan-fried fish like John Dory.

Or we would eat them at my friend Vittorio's restaurant in Portopalo after they had been roasted, sprinkled with oil and salt, in the ashes of the wood-burning stove, with each artichoke perched upright in a series of 'cones' forged into a special grill pan. When they came out, smoky and tender, you just peeled off the blackened outer leaves and ate the rest straight away. Artichokes are so important to the Sicilians that out of their season you could often find them in the supermarkets cleaned, cut into four and frozen, along with other vegetables, such as spinach, peas or broad beans.

Rome, too, has held a great importance in the development of artichokes in Italian cooking. Between January and May/June, artichokes and puntarelle are the two vegetables that are celebrated in Rome more than anywhere else in Italy. In the famous Campo di Fiori market you see the guys sitting at their tables taking beautiful purple and green artichokes from big baskets, and as they prepare them the outer leaves fall like petals into boxes at their feet. As they work they rub the cut artichokes with lemon juice and all you have to do is take them home and cook them.

When I am in Rome I always like to eat *carciofi alla giudìa* (artichokes Jewish-style). The special Romanesco artichokes grown in Lazio (which are very different to other varieties because they have no spikes) are pressed down and fried, with the stalk upwards, so that they open out and turn golden like Van Gogh's *Sunflowers*, then they are sprinkled with lemon juice and salt. There are famous restaurants in the Jewish quarter in Rome where the guys sit all day by the till, just like their counterparts in the market, turning boxes and boxes of artichokes, because everyone who comes in expects to eat *carciofi alla giudìa*.

The other famous Roman dish made with the same variety of artichokes is *carciofi alla Romana* (see the recipe on page 64) – artichokes braised whole with herbs – which makes a great starter, or you could double or triple the quantities for lunch or dinner. Any left over can be chopped and crushed in a pan and fried in olive oil until golden on both sides – you could even break in an egg, and add some grated Parmesan and salt and pepper, for a great starter.

Blanched or char-grilled artichokes kept under oil are also beautiful, but if you are buying them, check the labels to make sure that there is not too much sugar and salt added. I have also given a recipe for pickled artichokes on page 76.

Which to choose

There are actually around ninety different types of recognised artichoke, and every region has its local variety, with its own particular season, but most of them are never seen elsewhere. Some are entirely violet-purple, some green, some a mixture of both, depending on the areas of production, and in some regions a particular artichoke will have its own Protected Designation of Origin status, which means it must be grown to specific standards in a defined region by a member of a consortium of growers.

The best-known varieties can be roughly divided into three kinds:

The pointed baby Venetian artichokes, originally from the Laguna Veneto, are best sliced and baked, grilled or deep-fried (see page 65). The most famous are the stunning purple-violet variety which grow in the salty soil of the island of Sant' Erasmo, where the very first, tiniest, sought-after buds are called Castroere and are usually eaten raw. Venetian artichokes are also beautiful in risotto, under oil or pickled, especially served with burrata (see page 76).

Sardinian and Sicilian Spinoso (spiny) artichokes are more compact, slim and spiky. These are the ones that Vittorio cooks whole in ash using his special grill. They are great all-rounders, so you could use them for any of the recipes that follow, though Romanesco are better for cooking *alla Romana*.

Romanesco (which are also called Cimarolo or Mamole) and the Venetian Chioggia are more tender, flatter on the base and are best cooked with their stalk intact, as this is also delicious to eat. These are the varieties of artichoke to cook *alla Romana* (see page 64), They are also good raw, with Parmesan, and lemon oil, as in the recipe overleaf.

The only problem, sometimes, is finding the right wine to pair with artichokes, as their tannins and metallic, iron-y nature can make it quite complicated.

How to prepare
'Turning' or preparing an artichoke is a little fiddly, but not difficult. The thing to remember is that artichokes discolour very quickly, so once you cut them, they need to go straight into water that has been acidulated with lemon juice.

Have ready a big bowl of cold water. Cut a lemon in half, squeeze the juice into the water, then put the halves of lemon in, too. Then as you work, you can either dip the artichoke into the lemon water or just use the halved lemons to rub directly onto the exposed surfaces.

Hold the artichoke in one hand, then work your way around it snapping off and discarding the hard outer leaves from the base, until you reach the tender, yellow leaves underneath. Now cut off the bottom of the stalk, and with a small paring knife, trim off the stringy outside part all the way around the stalk, back to the core. Trim and scrape away the hard pieces around the base of each artichoke. Finally trim off the spiky tops of each of the leaves that are left using a sharp knife and then slice across the very top of the artichoke – take off about 2cm – enough to remove the spiky tops and reveal the choke inside.

Because the artichoke is actually a flower bud, the most important thing for it to do is to put out its seeds, so even when it is cut by its stalk from the plant, the choke – or beard, as I call it – will continue to grow, trying to develop into a flower. If the artichoke has been freshly harvested, or if it is very small, the choke will barely have formed, but the longer the artichoke has been cut from the plant, or the older or bigger it is, the more the choke will have developed and become hairy. So you need to scoop this out with a teaspoon. The easiest way to do this is to slice the artichokes in half lengthways first (unless the recipe calls for them to be left whole, as in *carciofi alla Romana* overleaf). As soon as the artichokes are sliced in half and the chokes removed, keep them in the acidulated water until you are ready to use them as they are, or cut them again into quarters or smaller pieces, according to your recipe.

Each recipe overleaf serves 6.

Raw with rocket, Parmesan and lemon oil
This can be a starter or a salad.

1 Take 6 medium artichokes and prepare as on the previous page. Cut in half lengthways, then using a mandoline or a very sharp knife, shave the artichokes lengthways as thinly as possible and put them into a bowl. Squeeze some more lemon juice over them straight away to avoid further discoloration. **2** Add 2 good handfuls of rocket, 2 tablespoons of grated Parmesan, 2 tablespoons of extra virgin olive oil and season. Toss all together and finish with some shavings of Parmesan.

Alla Romana (braised)
You need a variety of artichoke such as Romanesco, with a large base. The herb to use, if you can find it, is the Italian minty *mentuccia* (sometimes called *nepitella* or calamint).

1 Finely chop 3 cloves of garlic, and if you don't have any mentuccia, finely chop a handful of fresh mint leaves and a handful of parsley leaves, and mix with some sea salt and freshly ground black pepper and a touch of olive oil. Some people add some breadcrumbs and/or some chopped anchovies. **2** Prepare 6 medium artichokes as on the previous page but leave them whole, scoop out the choke with a teaspoon, then press the garlic and herb mixture into the hollow that you create. **3** Place upright in an ovenproof dish and add enough water to just cover them. Drizzle some more olive oil over the top and, if you like, a splash of white wine and a touch of vinegar (not too much vinegar, as they have already been in acidulated water). **4** Put in a bay leaf, a few peppercorns, and put into the oven at 160°C/gas 3 for 40 minutes, until the liquid is reduced and the artichokes are soft if you prick the heart with a toothpick. **5** Lift out and serve either hot or cold.

Carciofi fritti (fried)

Like the deep-fried courgettes on page 41, these are good to put out in a bowl with drinks.

1 Prepare 6 medium artichokes as for the recipe with rocket and Parmesan opposite, then toss the artichoke shavings in some semolina flour (for a more rustic appearance) or plain flour. **2** Heat some vegetable oil to 180°C in a deep-fryer or a large pan (no more than a third full). If you don't have a thermometer, drop in some flour and it should start to sizzle gently. **3** Deep-fry the flour-coated artichoke shavings until golden, then season with sea salt and freshly ground black pepper and sprinkle with a little lemon juice.

Caponata (sweet and sour)

1 Prepare 6 medium artichokes as on page 63, and cut into quarters. **2** Preheat the oven to 180°C/gas 4. **3** Bring 3 potatoes in their skins to the boil in salted water, then cook until just tender. Drain, and when cool enough to touch, peel and cut into cubes of about 1cm. **4** Spread 30g of pine nuts over a baking tray and put into the preheated oven for about 8 minutes until golden, then remove and chop. **5** Bring a pan of water to the boil with 70ml white wine vinegar, put in the artichoke quarters and blanch for a couple of minutes until just al dente, then lift out and drain. **6** Add a chopped stalk of celery to the water and repeat. **7** Heat a little olive oil in a sauté pan and put in the drained celery. Sauté until golden, then add the drained artichoke pieces along with a finely chopped clove of garlic and a few small fresh mint leaves, season with black pepper and stir for a few minutes. **8** Mix a tablespoon of sugar with a tablespoon of white wine vinegar in a cup, tip into the pan and bring to the boil, then turn down the heat, add the cubes of potato and the toasted pine nuts and take off the heat. **9** Cover with clingfilm and leave to cool down, so that the flavours can develop, before eating.

Winter vegetable stew

Ciambotta is the name that is often given to this stew of winter vegetables, which is a little more hearty and soupy than the spring vegetable dish of vignarola (see page 58) and makes a meal with chunks of bread or polenta. When Margherita was at school or home from university we would make up big batches of stews like this, using the vegetables that she could eat, then portion them up in bags in the freezer so she always had something she could take out and warm up to eat on its own or to have with some grilled chicken. You can use cabbage or kale instead of cavolo nero if you prefer.

1 Soak the beans in cold water overnight. 2 When ready to cook, drain the beans from their soaking water and put into a pan with the sage leaves. Cover with 1 litre of water, bring to the boil, then turn down the heat to a simmer for around 1 hour, until the beans are tender but still have a little bite. Take off the heat but leave in the pan. 3 Heat the olive oil in a large casserole dish, then add the onion, carrots, celery and bay leaves. Put on the lid and cook gently for 5 minutes, then put in the potatoes, season, and continue to cook gently for another 5 minutes. 4 Add the tomatoes, parsnips, squash and cavolo nero, then pour in half the cooking liquid from the pan of beans. Taste and adjust the seasoning if necessary, and continue to cook for another 10 minutes. 5 Discard the sage from the pan of beans, then add them to the casserole along with the rest of the cooking water. Check the seasoning again, simmer for 10 minutes, then serve.

Serves 6

dried cannellini beans 250g

fresh sage leaves 4

olive oil 3 tablespoons

white onion 2, cut into large dice

carrots 2, cut into large dice

celery 2 stalks

bay leaves 2

potatoes 2 large, cut into large dice

sea salt and freshly ground black pepper

ripe tomatoes 4 large, chopped

parsnips 2, cut into large dice

butternut squash ½, cut into large dice

cavolo nero 1 bunch, cut into large pieces

Grilled Jerusalem artichokes with heritage carrots

Jerusalem artichokes have an incredible sweet, nutty flavour and when they are griddled until they are crispy they are delicious, though as a child I also remember eating them raw, with my grandad, dipping them into *bagna cauda* (see page 55). Originally they were introduced to Italy and the rest of Europe from the New World, and one theory is that their name comes not from Jerusalem, the place, but the Italian word for sunflower, *girasole*, because they are actually a variety of sunflower. However, when the early explorers first found them, they needed to describe the flavour, which they likened to an artichoke.

Carrots have their own fascinating history, because the very first ones, which were grown in Afghanistan in around AD7, were purple, and later yellow, not orange at all, and they were long, thin and pointed. It is said that the purple ones began to lose favour around the Middle Ages because, a bit like beetroot, their colour came out into the cooking water and stained the pots. Then, around the sixteenth and seventeenth centuries, the Dutch developed the fatter, orange carrot that we all know today. Unfortunately, over time, for the sake of commercialisation, many varieties have been bred for appearance and resistance to disease, often hydroponically, and the flavour has been compromised, so that they either taste of very little, or they are so intensely sweet that they are barely recognisable as a carrot, which should have a much greater complexity of flavour and a hint of bitterness. It is a puzzle to me how carrots can often look so uniform, as if they were made by machine. I prefer my carrots ugly, but tasty!

Perhaps that frustration with bland carrots is why so much interest has been shown in heritage varieties, which are again being grown in their original colours and which have so much more flavour. If you can't find them, try to buy organic carrots, and if they have a bit of mud and greenery attached to them when you buy them, so much the better.

1 Cook the artichokes in boiling salted water for about 1 hour (depending on the size), until tender but still firm. Drain under cold water to stop them cooking further, then peel and slice 1cm thick. Drizzle with 1 tablespoon of the olive oil, then season and put on a hot griddle pan or barbecue until marked. 2 Pour the vinegar into a dish, put in the artichokes, cover with clingfilm and leave to marinate for 2 hours, turning them every so often. Lift out of the vinegar (but reserve this). 3 Peel the carrots and then, still using the peeler, shave into long strips. Put into a bowl of iced water to crisp up for about 10 minutes. Drain, season and put into a bowl. Toss with the reserved vinegar and the rest of the olive oil, then add the pea shoots. 4 Arrange the artichokes in a serving dish with the carrots and pea shoots on top.

Serves 6

Jerusalem artichokes	1kg, large
sea salt and freshly ground black pepper	
extra virgin olive oil	80ml
Pinot Grigio or other subtle white wine vinegar	150ml
golden, white and purple heritage carrots	200g of each
pea shoots	300g

Parma ham with peaches, walnuts and almonds

Parma ham has such a special place in the heart of a northern Italian; that noble, salty sweetness is so much a part of that set of flavours that we identify with our region, especially my generation, born in the sixties, when to have Parma ham was still considered special. I remember my grandad saying, 'You don't know how lucky you are to have it,' because there used to be no Parma ham for anyone outside the production area, and if you could find some, it was too expensive. So for us it was a symbol of the new Italy that was working to feed everyone. That meant applying a level of modernity and logistics to the curing and ageing process, so that where for hundreds of years you had been reliant on the weather and the specific microclimate around Parma, now you could control the temperature and the conditions.

When you went to people's houses sometimes they would serve Parma ham with figs, melon or mozzarella, or sometimes tomatoes – though personally I don't think tomatoes work: I prefer to add sweetness, rather than acidity, to the saltiness of the ham. And actually, although I like the combination of ham and ripe figs, cheese or melon, I always thought that in truth you couldn't make the ham taste better than it did just on its own, until someone suggested putting it out with peaches, almonds and walnuts. What can I say? I was completely shocked, because I realised that, actually, yes, you can make the ham taste even better. But of course the peaches have to be absolutely at their peak: perfectly ripe and juicy.

This isn't a real recipe, just an arrangement of brilliant ingredients.

1 Preheat the oven to 180°C/gas 4. **2** Lay the almonds and walnuts on separate baking trays and put into the oven for 7 minutes, moving the trays around occasionally so that the nuts turn golden all over. **3** Remove the trays from the oven and allow to cool slightly. **4** Rub the skins off the walnuts and roughly chop. Roughly chop the almonds. **5** Arrange the slices of ham in a shallow dish. **6** Cut the peaches in half, remove the stones, and cut each half into 8 slices. **7** Arrange the peach slices on top of the ham. **8** Sprinkle the nuts over the top and finish with a drizzle of olive oil.

Serves 6

almonds 200g, skin on

walnuts 200g

Parma ham 24 slices

ripe peaches 4

extra virgin olive oil

Bresaola with sharon fruit, oil and balsamic vinegar

Our neighbour in Corgeno, Luisa, used to have a persimmon tree that some years was so laden with the bright orange fruit, which stayed on the tree until late autumn, that she had to give some away to everyone in the village who wanted it. The problem was that not many people seemed to like the quite special flavour and texture, which was so unlike any other local fruit, but my grandad used to put them out in boxes in the winter sun to continue ripening until they were completely soft, sweet and spicy and I was always fascinated by them.

This simple, but quite unusual combination brings together sweet sharon fruit – which is the most well-known variety of persimmon – and salty bresaola, the typical salumi of the Valtellina valley in Lombardy, where the beef is salted and then marinated in wine and herbs or spices and air-dried so that it becomes a rich red colour.

People always ask you as a chef how you came to put certain ingredients together for the first time, and you feel a big pressure to pinpoint a brilliant moment of creation! Of course sometimes there is a moment of pure inspiration, but the reality is that everything is a mix of the flavour palate you grow up with and the multicultural ideas that you soak up all around you. In this case it made perfect sense to me to put together two ingredients from my own region of Italy, but also, I love Japanese food – I feel that the Italians and Japanese share a penchant for purity and simplicity of flavours – and since persimmons are a favourite Japanese fruit, who knows if that was also in the back of my mind?

Only make this when you have sharon fruit that is absolutely ripe and squidgy though – you can tell by the touch. If the fruit feels hard, don't buy it, as it won't be sweet enough. And when it isn't available, I still look for something to put with bresaola that will give an element of sweetness and sharpness – in Valtellina it is usually eaten with olive oil and lemon juice. You could combine it with figs or goat's cheese, or a salad of rocket and Parmesan, with a touch of balsamic vinegar in each case. The boys in the kitchen were adamant that balsamic vinegar is the right one to use here – and they are right, but it is a vinegar I only ever use now and again, very sparingly, and then make sure that it is a good, authentic one made to traditional methods, so that it has depth and complexity as well as sweetness.

Again, this isn't a recipe as much as a serving suggestion.

1 Arrange the bresaola on a serving dish. 2 Remove the skin from the sharon fruits, scoop out the soft flesh and dot it on top of the bresaola. 3 Drizzle with the olive oil and vinegar and finish with black pepper.

Serves 6

bresaola 24 thin slices

sharon fruits 3 large

extra virgin olive oil
2 tablespoons

aged balsamic vinegar
1 tablespoon

freshly ground black pepper

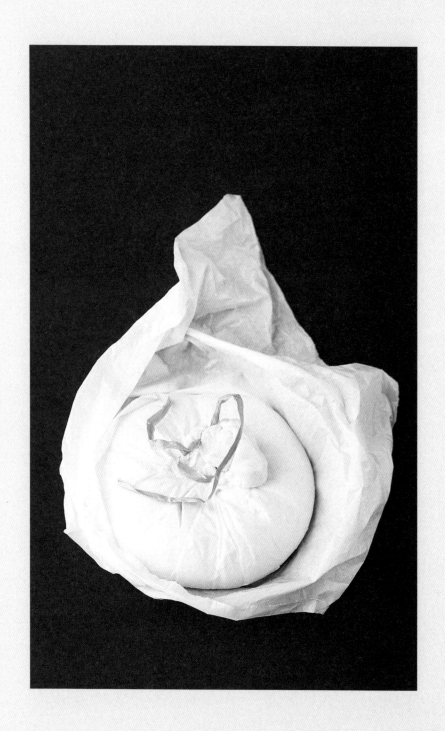

Burrata
x 4

Ah, the burrata revolution! It is incredible the way burrata
has captured the imagination in the last decade or so, when at
one time it was a cheese that nobody knew about, except the
people who worked in and around the creameries of Andria
in northern Puglia where cow's milk mozzarella is made –
because burrata began as a by-product of making mozzarella.
Mozzarella is made using the *pasta filata* technique (literally
'spun paste'), which involves putting the curds into a hot
water bath and kneading and stretching them, then forming
them into balls. The very elastic pieces of cheese that were
left behind after the mozzarellas were all made could be
stretched to make translucent white pouches, which were
filled with more small strings of the cheese mixed with cream,
which all melted togther. Then the pouches were wrapped
in the fresh green leaves of the asphodel plant. Burrata is a
fresh cheese that should preferably be eaten as soon as it
is made, but definitely within 2 or 3 days, and this was also
the life span of the leaves, so once they started to turn from
green to brown you would know that the cheese was no
longer good. These days the fresh leaves have been outlawed,
and the cheeses we buy today are sold in plastic versions.

It seems to me that because burrata has become so
fashionable and is less easily available than mozzarella,
people sometimes think that it must be a better cheese.
Not true. They are just different and shouldn't be judged
against each other. When you open a burrata it is incredibly
rich, sweet and buttery – hence the name, which is Italian
for butter – and as it is full of cream, I would say only eat it
occasionally and then really celebrate it. It makes a perfect
antipasti combined with the saltiness of cured meats such as
prosciutto, culatello (from the hind leg of the pig), capocollo
(cured neck) and some toasted focaccia or good rustic white
bread, drizzled with extra virgin olive oil. As well as the ways
suggested on the following pages, I also like burrata just
sprinkled with pomegranate seeds and extra virgin olive oil,
or with vignarola (braised spring vegetables, see page 58).

Each recipe overleaf makes enough for 6 with
500g of burrata.

With semi-dried tomato and basil

1 Preheat the oven to 140°C/gas 1. **2** Cut 2kg of cherry tomatoes in half and lay them on a roasting tray. **3** Sprinkle with sea salt and freshly ground black pepper and put into the oven for around 2 hours, until the tomatoes have begun to shrink and are semi-dried. **4** Remove from the oven and leave to cool down. **5** Put into a bowl with a few leaves of fresh basil, and toss gently with 2 tablespoons of extra virgin olive oil and a tablespoon of red wine vinegar. **6** Transfer to a serving dish and place some burrata on top. Leave these whole, so that everyone can scoop up some along with the tomatoes.

With pickled artichokes

1 Prepare 6 medium artichokes (see page 63) and cut into strips lengthways. **2** Bring 500ml of white wine, 500ml of white wine vinegar and 500ml of water to the boil with a tablespoon of sea salt in a large pan. **3** Lift the artichokes from the acidulated water, add to the pan and blanch for 5 minutes, then drain and keep to one side. (If you like, you can catch the liquid and store in the fridge in a plastic container to use next time). **4** Make a marinade by heating 250ml of extra virgin olive oil very gently in a pan with a black peppercorn, a juniper berry, a bay leaf, a couple of fresh sage leaves, a small sprig of fresh rosemary and a lightly crushed clove of garlic. As soon as the herbs begin to fry lightly and the garlic begins to change colour, switch off the heat, leave for 5 minutes to cool down a little, then carefully stir in 50ml of white wine vinegar. **5** Add the reserved artichokes and leave to cool down completely, before serving with burrata. If you prepare more pickled artichokes than you need, you can store them in a sterilised jar in the fridge, covered with a layer of olive oil, for up to a month.

With chicory, anchovy and chilli

If you can't find catalogna (wild chicory), you can use puntarelle leaves, which appear from November to March. At other times of the year you could substitute Swiss chard leaves.

1 Rinse 3 salted anchovies and dry them. Run your thumb gently along the backbone of each anchovy – this will allow you to easily pull it out and separate the fish into 6 fillets. **2** You need around 2kg of chicory or chard leaves. Wash these in plenty of cold water, then blanch for 2 minutes in boiling salted water until just tender, and drain. **3** Heat some olive oil in a pan, add 2 finely chopped cloves of garlic, 2 finely chopped hot red chillies and the anchovies, sauté until the garlic is golden, then add the leaves and sauté until any residual water has evaporated. **4** Add 3 tablespoons of white wine vinegar and cook for another 2 minutes, then take off the heat and leave to cool down. **5** Serve with burrata.

With roast butternut squash and hazelnuts

1 Preheat the oven to 180°C/gas 4. **2** Scatter 3 tablespoons of blanched hazelnuts over a baking tray and put into the preheated oven for about 7 minutes, moving the tray around occasionally so that the nuts become golden all over. **3** Remove the tray from the oven and allow the nuts to cool. **4** Turn up the oven to 220°C/gas 7. **5** Peel a butternut squash, then slice it in half lengthways, remove the seeds, then cut it lengthways into slices of about 1cm wide. **6** Lay the strips in a baking tin with a whole clove of garlic and a sprig of thyme and put into the oven for about 20 minutes, until the squash has caramelised. **7** Remove and leave to cool, then cut each strip crossways into dice. **8** Toss with 2 tablespoons of Giorgio's dressing (see page 19). **9** Roughly chop the hazelnuts and sprinkle over the top together with a few leaves of fresh thyme. Serve with burrata.

When I was growing
up my grandad used
to tell us that if you
wanted to know
something about the
character of your
neighbours, you
just had to look into
their soup. He would
say about a family
that lived in the
village, 'Don't trust
them, those guys
put parsley in their
minestrone.'

Simple soups

Chilled tomato soup with whipped ricotta

This is a soup to make in the summer when you have plenty of almost over-ripe tomatoes; one for hot days and parties when you can have a big jug of it in the fridge ready to pour. If you mention cold soup, people think straight away of the Spanish gazpacho, but these soups are all over Europe. The addition of ricotta is what gives it a lift and makes it a bit more special, and also I would say this recipe has more pure tomato-sweetness, and is a little less aggressive than some gazpachos that are made with peppers as well as tomato – but if you want to add a little chilli, that is fantastic too. Like most soups it is best made the day before you want to eat it. The use of a good extra virgin olive oil is very important. Preferably use a fruity southern Italian oil, but even if you use a strong Tuscan one, the acidity of the tomato will always help you out by neutralising the strong flavour of the oil a little.

We use shorter Italian cucumbers, which tend to be less watery and have a more distinctive flavour.

1 Put the tomatoes and cucumber into a blender with the olive oil and chopped mint and blend until smooth, then pass through a fine sieve into a bowl. Taste and season, then put into the fridge for 3–4 hours. **2** In a separate bowl, whisk the ricotta with the chives. **3** Ladle the soup into individual bowls, then drop in small teaspoonfuls of the ricotta. **4** Garnish each bowl with mint leaves and half a cherry tomato.

Serves 6

ripe cherry tomatoes 1.2kg, plus 3 for garnish

cucumber 1, peeled and cut into chunks

extra virgin olive oil 200ml

chopped fresh mint leaves 2 teaspoons, plus some whole leaves for garnish

sea salt and freshly ground black pepper

fresh ricotta 150g

chopped fresh chives 2 teaspoons

Pumpkin soup with black rice and prawns

This is the soup I make when I am on my own at home. I drop into the supermarket or the organic market next to our house and whatever I plan to buy, I always come out with a pumpkin. I love the sweetness of the soup on its own, just with croutons and some grated Parmesan, but the addition of the prawns and rice elevates it into something smarter, for when you want to serve it for friends.

Most pumpkin and squash is good for soup as long as it is ripe and isn't too watery. A ripe pumpkin will be quite heavy, with a strong sweet smell at the base, and when you tap it, it will have a hollow sound. Crown Prince is excellent, if you can find it, but butternut squash is good too.

Don't throw away the seeds, as you can roast them in the oven, season them, and snack on them. My grandfather was aggressively against wasting any food, so whenever my grandmother cooked pumpkin he would dry the seeds outside on pieces of wood, then sow some in the garden so we had pumpkins the following year, but he would keep some back which my grandmother tossed in a little bit of olive oil and salt. So tasty, and good for you.

You could also use cooked prawns in this, but you don't need to sauté them first. Just drop them into the boiling soup and make sure they are hot all the way through before serving.

Black rice adds a bit of drama, but if you don't have any, you could use some organic long-grain rice and cook for the time stated on the packet instead.

1 Preheat the oven to 170°C/gas 3. **2** Cut the pumpkin or squash in half, then in half again, but leave the skin on. Scrape out the seeds (you can roast these separately if you like). **3** Pour some water into a roasting tin – to about 1cm deep. Season the pumpkin or squash and put into the tin. Cover with foil and put into the preheated oven for 1½ hours, then take off the foil and bake for a further 20 minutes, until the pumpkin is very soft.

4 Meanwhile, cook the rice in boiling salted water for 45 minutes, until just tender, then drain. **5** Heat a tablespoon of olive oil in a frying pan and sauté the rice until crispy. Scoop out the rice, keep to one side and clean the pan ready to cook the prawns. **6** Scrape the pumpkin or squash flesh from the skin and put it into a blender, discarding the skin. Add the double cream and blitz briefly, then add enough stock to blend to a smooth, velvety soup. How much stock you use will depend on the texture of the pumpkin, and how thick you like the soup to be, so you may not need it all. Return the soup to the pan and bring to the boil, then turn down to a simmer.

7 Meanwhile, heat the rest of the oil in the frying pan, and when hot put in the prawns. Season and sauté briefly until they change colour and are cooked through. **8** Pour the soup into warmed bowls and garnish with the rice and prawns.

Serves 6

pumpkin such as Crown Prince, or butternut squash 1

sea salt and freshly ground black pepper

black rice 100g

olive oil 2 tablespoons

double cream 150ml

good vegetable stock 1–1.5 litres

raw king prawns, cleaned and de-veined 18

Pappa pomodoro
(Tuscan tomato soup)

I have a really strong memory from when I was growing up of a singer called Rita Pavone, who was very popular in the sixties and had a song called *'Viva la Pappa col Pomodoro'*: 'Viva la pa-pa-pap-pa; Col po-po-po-po-po-po- Pomodoro...' In those days Italian songs always seemed to be about our mothers or the food we ate. I remember telling my grandad, 'I want to have this pappa pomodoro in the song,' and he would say, 'You don't want that, it is something southern people eat.'

This is a beautiful soup that manages to be both contemporary and nostalgic – actually it is so thick that it is barely a soup at all, more like a rustic purée. When I eat it, it feels like taking a step back in time, but it has a really strong message about food that is very relevant now, because its essence is the frugality of using up stale bread and over-ripe tomatoes. It reminds me of *la scarpeta*, the scrap of bread you use to mop your plate at the end of your spaghetti in tomato sauce – but it is so full of flavour and for me a little cupful can be as elegant as a spoonful of caviar. I remember going to a very smart fund-raising party in the height of the summer at the River Cafe, where they were serving it in cups; just the tomato soup, without the egg. My good friend and chef, Fergus Henderson, and I must have eaten half a dozen each. Every time the waiters brought the trays of it round, the soup looked so oily and shiny and inviting, Fergus would say, 'It's winking at us,' so we had another one, and another one, and another. What I especially loved was to look around at a roomful of millionaires tucking into this beautiful dish that was also the staple diet of a Tuscan farmer.

I must admit I like the addition of poached eggs, especially when I want to make it more of a meal. I just turn off the heat under the pan of soup at the end of the cooking time, break in the eggs, put the lid on the pan and leave it for about 7 minutes, until the whites of the eggs have cooked but the yolks are still soft. Sometimes when Plaxy and I are on holiday and we get up late and there is some pappa pomodoro

left over from the evening before, I will re-heat it, break some eggs into it like this, and that is brunch. I always like to keep back a little of the toasted bread to put in at the end, so that the soup has a fantastic soft consistency from the bread you cook into it, but then you just have a little contrasting crunch on top. You want a sturdy, white, crusty country bread or sourdough – the perfect one is the traditional unsalted Tuscan bread – and the olive oil is also pivotal: you need a powerful, southern sunshine oil, not a more reserved one from the north. The touch of vinegar is also important, to balance the flavours, so you can adjust it as you prefer, and don't be scared to kick the flavour even more with some extra garlic and plenty of pepper.

Pappa pomodoro (see picture on previous page)
1 Preheat the oven to 180°C/gas 4. **2** Lay the cubes of bread on a baking tray and toast in the preheated oven until golden (move the cubes around occasionally so that they are coloured on all sides). **3** Heat half the olive oil in a large pan, then add the onion, garlic, carrot, celery and chilli. Cook gently until the onion is soft and translucent, then add the tomatoes and continue to cook gently for 30 minutes. Add the vinegar and the toasted bread (keeping back a few cubes, to serve, if you like) and cook for a further 25–30 minutes, until the soup has a quite thick, rustic consistency. **4** Taste and season as necessary, then ladle into warmed bowls. Swirl in the rest of the olive oil and scatter in some basil and the reserved toasted bread, if using.

Serves 6

good, stale country bread or sourdough 400g, cubed

extra virgin olive oil 200ml

onion 1, chopped about 1cm

garlic 1 clove, finely chopped

carrot 1, chopped about 1cm

celery 1 stalk, chopped about 1cm

chopped mild red chilli
1 tablespoon

ripe plum tomatoes 2kg, chopped

red wine vinegar 1 tablespoon

sea salt and freshly ground black pepper

fresh basil leaves 100g

Chestnut soup with spelt

This is a slightly more sophisticated version of a traditional soup, which I like to finish with spelt and aromatic oil.

Chestnuts are so important to northern Italians. I possibly even owe my existence to them, as without chestnuts and chestnut flour, which was like gold dust to families deprived of wheat flour during the war, many families would have struggled to survive. They were so vital in my region that my grandad remembered a time when you risked being shot if you trespassed on someone's land to raid their trees, because you were taking food from their mouths. Some enterprising people used to string the nuts into 'crowns', make a fire and hang them over it to dry them out, then they would sell them. My grandmother used to soak the dried chestnuts overnight in water, then cook them very, very slowly in milk to make a beautiful, simple soup. The milk would be bought fresh that morning, topped with so much cream you had to shake it, and the chestnuts would plump up and then break apart. That soup was one of my absolute favourite things. My grandmother would start it off in the afternoon when my brother and I were at school, and when we came home, as soon as we walked through the door the smell of it cooking was incredible.

Up in the wooded mountains above Corgeno, where there was no grass, so no possibility of straw, even the leaves of the chestnut trees were important, as they could be collected when they fell and used as bedding for the animals.

When I was growing up, most of the activities in the village revolved around the oratorium, the grassy area below the church, where we played football and other games, and once a year we would all go up into the mountains with the priest to collect the chestnuts, bring them back down to the oratorium, and there would be a big party while the chestnuts roasted in pans with holes in the base over an open fire. It was one of my favourite things to be in charge of the fire. We would lay down an empty potato sack and on top we would have some of the big, woody

outer leaves that you pull from the Savoy cabbages
when they splay out after the first frost. The trick
was to take some chestnuts from the fire, wrap them
in the leaves, then close them up in the sack and
roll it quickly back and forth. If you did it properly
the heat and humidity would peel off the shells like
magic, the slight steaminess would keep them soft
and the sweet smell of the nuts was incredible.

In a generation, though, I feel the old attachment
to chestnuts, especially in soups and baking, has
gone, perhaps because the older people don't want
to eat something that reminds them of the days when
they were very poor, and the younger generation
have never really been introduced to them, except
as marrons glacés, the candied nuts you have at
Christmas.

Personally I think chestnuts are delicious,
very healthy, and I love this soup, which is a more
contemporary version, and of course you can make it
with vacuum-packed chestnuts, if you prefer.

Chestnut soup with spelt

1 Preheat the oven to 200°C/gas 6. **2** If using whole chestnuts, score a cross into the top of each one with a sharp knife and lay them in a roasting tray (if you like, you can scatter a little sea salt over the tray first, as it adds a little flavour to the nuts as they roast). Put into the oven for 10 minutes, until the skin colours and crisps up and starts to pull away from the flesh. Transfer to a bowl and cover with a clean tea towel so that they steam a little – this makes them easier to peel. When they are cool enough to handle, peel and chop them. If using vacuum-packed chestnuts, simply chop them. **3** Heat 2 tablespoons of the olive oil in a pan. Add the onion, celery, carrot and pancetta and cook gently until the onion is soft and translucent. Add the bulk of the chestnuts (keeping back about a quarter for garnish) and sauté for a couple of minutes, then season, add the stock and cook gently for 20 minutes.

4 Meanwhile, cook the spelt in boiling salted water for about 12 minutes, until it is tender but still has a little bite to it. Take off the heat, drain and transfer to a bowl, then drizzle with another tablespoon of the olive oil. **5** To make the aromatic oil, pour the extra virgin olive oil into a pan and add the rest of the ingredients. Heat gently until the oil barely starts to bubble (80–90°C if you have a kitchen thermometer). Allow to infuse like this for 10 minutes, then pour through a fine sieve, squashing down the garlic, tomatoes, herbs and peppercorns with a ladle, to force as much flavour as possible into the oil.

6 Transfer about 3 ladlefuls of the soup at a time to a blender together with a ladle of the infused oil, and blend until silky and emulsified. Don't be tempted to add more oil in one go, or the soup may split. Transfer each batch to a warmed serving bowl, while you blend the rest in the same way. **7** Ladle into warmed bowls and garnish with some of the spelt and the reserved chestnuts.

Serves 6

whole chestnuts 1kg whole when in season, or 800g vacuum-packed chestnuts

sea salt and freshly ground black pepper

olive oil 3 tablespoons

onion 1, chopped

celery 2 stalks, chopped

carrot 1, chopped

pancetta 2 slices, chopped

chicken stock 2 litres

spelt 200g

For the aromatic oil:

extra virgin olive oil 200ml

garlic 3 cloves, whole

large tomatoes 2, halved

fresh rosemary 2 sprigs

black peppercorns 1 teaspoon

bay leaves 2

Spinach soup with poached eggs

This was always an important standby soup in our house, because Margherita could eat spinach – though we had to make it for her without the eggs. For that reason, I am a fan of frozen spinach – it is one of those vegetables that takes very well to freezing, so we always have a bag of it at home. In this recipe we use double cream, but it is also good without it.

So many of the simple soups I grew up with can be elevated to a whole meal by adding a poached egg, which breaks up voluptuously into the soup as you eat it.

You can either poach the eggs freshly just before you serve the soup, or, to make life easier, cook them in advance and lift them carefully out of the pan and into a bowl of iced water. Then, when you are ready to serve the soup, lift one into each bowl and ladle the hot soup over the top. If you like you can also toast a slice of bread for each person and put it into the soup bowl first, then put the egg on top.

Everybody has their own 'special' way to poach eggs that they think is the best. My way is to bring a large pan of water to the boil – I would use 2 or 3 litres for 6 eggs – and add 1 tablespoon of white wine vinegar. It is best to poach the eggs in two batches. Turn down the heat so that only a few bubbles break the surface. Break each egg into a cup, then stir the water to create a little whirlpool and slide the egg into the centre of it, so that the white of the egg folds around the yolk, instead of becoming wispy. Poach very, very gently for 4–5 minutes, depending on the size of the egg.

1 Heat the olive oil in a pan, add the shallots and cook gently until soft and translucent, then add the butter and spinach and as soon as it wilts, season to taste. Add the double cream and half the vegetable stock and bring to the boil, then take off the heat straight away. This is very important, because if you cook the spinach for too long it will start to oxidise, turning dark and taking on a tinny flavour, when you want it to be bright green and fresh. **2** Transfer the contents of the pan to a blender and blend until smooth (again, do this as briefly as possible, in order to retain the colour), adding more stock as necessary until you have the consistency you want. **3** Put a poached egg into each warmed bowl and ladle the soup around it.

Serves 6

olive oil	1 tablespoon
shallots	5 large, finely chopped
unsalted butter	50g
fresh green spinach	1.5kg
sea salt and freshly ground black pepper	
double cream	100ml
good hot vegetable stock	2 litres

To serve:

poached eggs (see opposite) 6

Pancotto:
'Get well' bread soup
x 4

Sometimes people seem to be reluctant to buy a big loaf of country bread or sourdough, because they think they won't eat it all, but there are so many things you can do with leftover bread. I believe that we have a responsibility to buy bread that is properly made from a few simple ingredients, time and patience, not processed so quickly that it becomes indigestible. A baker should be almost as important as the doctor to the local community, someone with a face and a name and a smile, who makes bread that is good and nutritious for all our families. And to me it is a celebration of such bread to use the stale pieces to make a comforting restorative soup, a tradition you find all over Italy, where to throw away bread is seen as a crime.

The recipe varies according to the style of bread and the produce of the region but essentially these are the soups you made when you had nothing else to eat, or you were feeling under the weather. I remember the first pancotto I tasted was made for me by the father of my very first girlfriend when I was a teenager in Corgeno, and it was full of garlic and chilli. He seemed quite exotic to us because he had travelled a great deal, his whole family was very artistic, and he was known for being a bit of a health guru and eating copious amounts of garlic, which he considered so good for him that he would even make a warm breakfast drink of garlic, chilli and olive oil. The joke was that after he bought his newspaper in the morning, they had to keep the door of the shop open all day to clear the air. But he was as strong as an ox, he used to windsurf with us when he was well into his seventies and he lived until he was ninety-seven, so there must have been something in it.

These are four of my favourite bread soups. Each recipe overleaf makes enough for 6.

With egg and cheese (from Pavese)

This is a soup steeped in legend, from the region of Lombardy where they tamed the Po river. It is said that before the French king, Francis I, was defeated by Charles V of Spain at the battle of Pavia in 1525, he took refuge in a local cottage where he asked the woman of the house for something to eat. All she had was a simple broth, but in order to make it more special for a king she fried some stale bread, put it into a bowl, broke an egg over it, ladled in the broth and grated in some cheese. The story goes that the king loved the soup so much that when he was eventually restored to his court it became a favourite.

1 You need 6 slices of country bread or sourdough and 200g of butter. **2** Fry 3 of the slices in half the butter until rich and golden, then lift out and repeat with the rest of the butter and the bread. Have ready 4 tablespoons of grated grana padano cheese.
3 Bring 1.5 litres of good beef stock to the boil in a large pan. **4** Put a slice of bread into each of six warmed bowls, add an egg yolk on top of each, then ladle in the stock. **5** Sprinkle with some of the cheese and finish with a good twist of black pepper.

With cavolo nero (from Tuscany)

Tuscan bread is unsalted, possibly because it would traditionally be eaten with the salty ham of the region. In Tuscany they have a wild mint called *nepitella*, or calamint, which is reminiscent of various different herbs rather than straightforwardly minty, and is often used with mushrooms as well as in this soup. You can find dried *nepitella*, or you can use a sprig of rosemary instead.

1 In a pan, heat 2 tablespoons of extra virgin olive oil, preferably a peppery Tuscan one, add 3 finely chopped cloves of garlic and a sprig of fresh rosemary (or a pinch of dried *nepitella*), and when the garlic is soft, but not coloured, add 200g of cavolo nero.
2 Sauté for 2 minutes, until the cabbage wilts a little. Add 1.5 litres of water and bring to the boil, then turn down to a simmer for 10 minutes. **3** Add 6 large slices, or 12 small slices, of stale white unsalted Tuscan bread, if you can find it, otherwise use country bread or sourdough. Simmer for another 5 minutes and when the bread begins to break up, taste and season with sea salt and freshly ground black pepper.
4 Have ready 2 more tablespoons of good, strong Tuscan oil and 200g of grated pecorino cheese. Ladle the soup into warmed bowls, sprinkle some cheese into each and drizzle with some of the olive oil.

With potato, rocket and chilli (from Puglia)

In Puglia the famous flagship bread of the region, *Pane di Altamura*, comes from the Bari province and has Protected Designation of Origin status, which dictates that it must be made with particular local varieties of hard durum wheat flour that give a yellow colour to the bread. The big rustic loaves are quite light, with a thick, crunchy crust and big air-holes inside, and are known for their ability to keep for up to two weeks, so shepherds could carry them on their journeys. As far back as 37BC, the Roman poet Horace wrote of the bread as the best to be had, especially for the 'wise traveller'. If you can't find Pugliese bread, use a baguette instead. The other particular characteristic of this soup is that there is no cheese involved.

1 Peel and chop 700g of potatoes (Desiree if possible) and cook in 1.5 litres of salted water for around 15 minutes until soft. **2** Add 500g of rocket and 4 thick slices of Pugliese bread or baguette. Taste and season with sea salt and freshly ground black pepper, then take off the heat. **3** In a pan, heat 100ml of extra virgin olive oil very gently, then add 2 finely chopped cloves of garlic and a finely chopped mild red chilli – you don't want to fry them, just let them infuse the oil for a few minutes. **4** Ladle the soup into warmed bowls and drizzle a little of the garlicky-chilli oil over the top.

With tomato and chilli (from Calabria)

Calabrian bread is similar to Tuscan bread but is made with salt, but you can use slices of country bread or sourdough. Chilli is synonymous with Calabria, so put in as much as you like. I like to finish the soup abundantly with olive oil.

1 Bring 1.5 litres of salted water to the boil in a pan. **2** Add 300g of chopped large tomatoes, such as San Marzano, 2 chopped stalks of celery, a chopped large hot red chilli (but preferably more, if you can take it), a handful of fresh basil leaves and 2 bay leaves, then turn down the heat and simmer for 30 minutes. **3** Add 6 large slices, or 12 small slices, of country bread or sourdough and simmer for a further 5 minutes. **4** Have ready 200g of grated pecorino cheese and 2 tablespoons of extra virgin olive oil. **5** Ladle the soup into warmed bowls and finish with a little cheese and a generous swirl of the olive oil.

Pasta fagioli (bean and pasta soup with mussels)

The idea of adding mussels to a bean and pasta soup gives a whole new lease of life to an old staple that many a country farmer's family would have fallen back on time and time again during the winter in the north of Italy: almost an equivalent of baked beans for the English. There are so many handed-down regional recipes for these kinds of soups, which inevitably start rows among Italians as to which is the most authentic. Wherever I travel I am always inquisitive about local ingredients and recipes, and when I was in Tuscany one time visiting some vineyards, the conversation turned to a particular bean soup, which sparked off a whole tirade about the way they made it in one of the neighbouring villages. Apparently it was an absolute insult, when the only difference was the addition of sage. That is how deep the sentiments about soup can run in Italy!

In this case I don't remember how we first came to add the marjoram, but its delicate, aromatic character bridges the flavours of the beans and the mussels perfectly. If you don't have any ditalini, you can use up broken bits of spaghetti, and you can add a dash of chilli oil at the end, if you like. In the summer it is also good if you allow the soup to cool down before serving.

To prepare mussels:
Scrub the shells really well under cold, running water, removing any beards. Discard any mussels that are open or that won't close if you tap them against your work surface. Once cooked, discard any that haven't opened.

If a recipe calls for clams, prepare them in the same way (though of course they don't have beards.)

1 Put the dried (or freshly podded) beans into a pan of cold water and bring to the boil. Turn down the heat and simmer for about 45 minutes–1 hour for fresh beans, and around 1–1½ hours for dried beans, until they are just soft. **2** Transfer three-quarters of the beans to a blender with a little of their cooking water (reserve the rest) and blend to a soup consistency. **3** Heat the olive oil in a separate pan, add the leeks, shallots, carrot and celery, and then the garlic and rosemary. Cook gently for 2 minutes, add the tomato purée and cook for another minute, then lift out the garlic and rosemary and discard them. **4** Add the reserved beans with their cooking water, along with the blended beans.

5 Put the mussels into a large pan with the wine, cover with a lid and cook over a high heat, shaking the pan a couple of times, until the mussels open, then take off the heat and keep to one side. Discard any that haven't opened, then shell around 15–20 of them, leaving the rest in their shells for garnish.

6 Cook the pasta in plenty of boiling salted water for about 2 minutes or according to the packet instructions, then drain and add to the bean soup along with the shelled mussels and some of the reserved cooking liquid. Transfer to a large, warmed serving bowl. Add the marjoram, taste and season. **7** Sit the mussels in their shells on top and garnish with the extra marjoram. Drizzle with extra virgin olive oil and finish with black pepper.

Serves 6

dried borlotti beans 800g, soaked overnight (or, if you can find them, 1.6kg fresh beans in their pods)

olive oil 100ml

leeks 2 medium, chopped

shallots 3, chopped

carrot 1, chopped

celery 2 stalks, chopped

garlic 3 cloves, whole

fresh rosemary 2 sprigs

tomato purée 1 tablespoon

mussels 800g, cleaned (see opposite)

white wine ½ glass (35ml)

small pasta, such as ditalini 500g

sea salt and freshly ground black pepper

fresh marjoram leaves 2 tablespoons, plus a little extra for garnish

a little extra virgin olive oil

Pasatelli with Parmesan cream and Parma ham

In Ferrara, in Emilia-Romagna, they say that even if life gets very bad, if you have a dish of *pasatelli* for dinner you will have a good night. This is a typical soup from this region of northern Italy, made with fat worm-like dumplings (a bit like the German *spaetzle*) of cheese, breadcrumbs and egg, cooked in chicken stock so that they puff up. Everyone will tell you they make *pasatelli* better than anyone else. I remember our former head chef, Federico, and his wife Benedetta would always argue about it. He would say the ones his family made in Tuscany were the best. She would say no way were they as good as the ones made by her grandmother. I like the *pasatelli* in the traditional way, just served in the chicken stock, with some grated Parmesan over the top: it is such a bowlful of warm, generous goodness. But we also put a twist on it with this version, in which we lift the *pasatelli* out of the stock once they are cooked and serve them with a Parmesan cream (don't waste the chicken stock, though: you can filter it and keep it in the freezer for another time).

You need one of those ingenious potato ricers with large holes to press the mixture through into the stock, which does need to be very good flavourful chicken stock, and it must be just under boiling, or you will destroy the dumplings. There shouldn't be too many of them either; they should just 'swim' around in the stock. We like a touch of lemon zest in the dumpling mixture, and the addition of nutmeg is also very important.

1 In a bowl mix the breadcrumbs, Parmesan and eggs, then mix in the lemon zest and nutmeg and work into a firm dough. **2** Heat the olive oil in a sauté pan, add the Parma ham strips and fry until crispy. Lift out and drain on kitchen paper. **3** For the Parmesan cream, bring the cream to the boil in a pan and cook until reduced by half. Add the Parmesan and keep stirring until the cheese has melted. Keep warm. **4** Bring the chicken stock to the boil in a separate pan, then put the dough into the potato ricer and squeeze it into the stock, slicing it off with a wet knife every 4–5 cm or so (any longer and the dumplings may break). Simmer gently for 2–3 minutes, until the dough puffs up. **5** Meanwhile, spoon some of the Parmesan cream into each of six warmed bowls, then, with a slotted spoon, lift out the dumplings and divide between the bowls. Finish with the Parma ham crisps.

Serves 6

breadcrumbs, made from stale bread 240g

Parmesan 240g, grated

eggs 6

lemon finely grated zest of 1

nutmeg 1 teaspoon, grated

olive oil 1 tablespoon

sliced Parma ham 150g, cut crossways into strips

good chicken stock 3 litres

For the Parmesan cream:

double cream 200ml

Parmesan 250g, grated

I love the idea that
the panini and the
pasties and pies
that centuries
ago travellers and
shepherds would
carry with them into
the mountains are
the same things we
still make at home,
so that there is
always something for
a wholesome snack.

Panini, crostini, pies and other snacks

Erbazzone

This is the kind of simple savoury 'green' pie that you see cut into squares and put out in the bars in Emilia-Romagna. It is such an easy thing to make, and the ingredients for the filling are so humble, in a way, that there is something very gratifying about how delicious it tastes when it comes out of the oven – it is perfect for breakfast, mid-morning, lunch or afternoon, and it is even better the day after you have baked it.

There are variations all over Italy, often with their own regional names. The particular greens or herbs that are mixed with ricotta and Parmesan inside the pastry are what determine the character and reflect the produce from the region where they are made. When I was filming in Liguria we made *torta pasqualina*, a local version that also has eggs baked inside it, using masses of the wild mountain herbs – some that I had never seen before – that we picked with a lady called Maria, who was 78 years old and still climbed up the steep stepped slopes every day to collect them. She had an incredible, encyclopedic knowledge of local herbs passed down to her by her grandmother. I made two pies with the herbs and I knew they were good when the director said, 'It's a wrap' at the end of filming and the crew dived on them and devoured them in minutes.

The recipe here features spinach and chard, rather than herbs, but these are interchangeable with any greens that are in season: even nettles, though I would always mix these with some spinach, otherwise the flavour could be too strong. I like the addition of pancetta, but you can leave it out for a vegetarian pie. Likewise, we use *strutto* (lard) for the pastry, but you could make it with olive oil, or half butter and half oil.

1 In a bowl mix together the flour, yeast, lard or olive oil and enough warm water to make a firm and smooth dough. 2 Preheat the oven to 200°C/gas 6. 3 Blanch the spinach or Swiss chard, or both, in salted, boiling water for about a minute, then drain and chop. 4 Heat some olive oil in a pan, add the pancetta (if using), shallots and garlic and cook until the shallots are soft and translucent, then mix in the spinach and/or chard. 5 Transfer all the ingredients to a bowl and leave to cool, then stir in the ricotta and Parmesan and season to taste. 6 Divide the dough in two and roll each piece out into a circle 5mm thick. 7 Lay one circle of dough in a round roasting tin, spread the ricotta mixture over the top and cover with the other circle of dough. Pinch the edges together. 8 Put the pie into the preheated oven and bake for 30 minutes, until golden. 9 Five minutes before the end of the baking time, brush with a little more olive oil.

Serves 6

00 flour 400g

fresh yeast 15g

strutto (lard) 100g, or 100ml olive oil

spinach or Swiss chard (or a mixture) 1kg

sea salt and freshly ground black pepper

olive oil a little extra for sautéing and to finish

pancetta 75g, diced (optional)

shallots 200g, chopped

garlic 1 clove, chopped

fresh ricotta 600g

Parmesan 100g, grated

Milanese and gremolata panini

My mum still says that she makes the best chicken *milanese*. When I phone her, she will tell me that someone in the village wasn't well, so she took them a *milanese* and 'now they are feeling better already.'

Thin slices of chicken, veal or pork, passed through some egg, flour and breadcrumbs and pan-fried, were so much the story of my childhood and my teenage years. While Plaxy would have been out in London watching bands like The Clash, I was at home in Corgeno eating *scallopini*, the affectionate word for the little pieces of meat that my mother and grandmother would buy from the butcher in the village. They would make two or three *scaloppini* each for me and my brother when we came home from school, and we would always be reminded how lucky we were to have them. That was the message, after the war, that to have any meat at all was a sign of wealth. It is not that long ago, and yet if I tell that to Jack or Margherita they look at me as if to say, 'What are you talking about?'

The *milanese* were also one of the many examples of the importance of saving leftover bread. My grandmother would have any that didn't go into soup drying beside the oven, and then she would grate it into crumbs which were kept in jars: some very fine ones for meatballs, and some bigger ones for mixing with herbs to coat fish before baking it. The ones that were for the *milanese* were put into the oven to dry out and take on a little colour.

The Italian boys in the kitchen at Locanda have the same attachment to *milanese*, so they must have it once a week when they all sit down to eat before the evening service. I like *milanese* every way, but topped with some gremolata and sandwiched inside some focaccia, it is a brilliant snack. In Milan, you see sandwiches like this under glass on the counter of every bar, or being sold from stalls in the markets.

If you want to make your own focaccia, use the recipe on pages 128-9, but omit the cherry tomatoes.

1 To make the gremolata, on a chopping board crush the garlic into a paste with the back of a large knife. 2 Chop the parsley on top so that they mix together, add the lemon zest and mix well. Keep to one side. 3 Put the slices of veal or chicken between two sheets of clingfilm and flatten with a meat hammer or the end of a rolling pin until about 6mm thick. 4 Have the flour and eggs in separate shallow bowls. 5 Mix the Parmesan and breadcrumbs together in another shallow bowl and season.

6 Pass each slice of veal or chicken through the flour, so that it is just lightly dusted. Lift up with a fork and dip into the egg, then the Parmesan and breadcrumbs. Press this coating on to the meat so that it is completely covered. 7 Heat some oil in a large sauté pan, put in the coated veal or chicken and sauté until golden on each side. Lift out and drain on kitchen paper. 8 Cut the focaccia into six squares and slice each one in half horizontally. 9 Spoon some gremolata on top of each slice of veal or chicken and sandwich between the slices of focaccia.

Makes 6 panini

silverside of rose veal or chicken breast 6 slices

plain flour 200g

eggs 3, beaten with a little sea salt and freshly ground black pepper

Parmesan 100g, grated

dried breadcrumbs 400g

sea salt and freshly ground black pepper

sunflower or seed oil for frying

plain focaccia 1

For the gremolata:

garlic 2 cloves

fresh parsley a small bunch

lemons grated zest of 2

Crostini
x 4

The name crostini comes from the Italian *crosta*, meaning crust, and it is born of the Italian philosophy that to throw away bread is one of the worst things you can do.

One of the greatest things, if you are out camping, is to toast pieces of bread that have become a little dry, on a fork over the fire, then just rub them with a clove of garlic and a little olive oil. There is something so elemental and earthy and delicious about eating bread like this in the open air. Or you can turn slices of a leftover loaf into a colourful snack or canapé to have with a drink. People ask what is the difference between crostini and bruschetta – well, sometimes these days there is not so much. I would say crostini is always of a size that you can eat with your fingers and traditionally was more of a northern Italian thing, made with plain toasted bread; whereas bruschetta was originally made with the big breads that are typical of southern Italy which would be sliced, toasted and rubbed with tomato, olive oil and garlic. But there are no rules any more, so you can also have crostini that is rubbed with oil, garlic and tomato, and when you have perfect ripe tomatoes it can be fabulous just as it is, without any additional topping.

If you want to be more adventurous, I would say there are no real limits to what you can put on a crostini, though I love the idea that a particular version reflects the bread and the ingredients of a certain area and becomes a special thing of pride: for example, crostini topped with hot chicken livers in Tuscany, or salt cod or marinated fish in the Veneto. One of my favourites (overleaf) is something I found myself making at home when I had sliced a fillet of beef into steaks for friends and had some left over, so I decided to turn it into a topping for crostini to have alongside. It is just very finely chopped raw beef, shallot, anchovy and capers: a simpler, less rich version of the classic French steak tartare.

Each recipe overleaf makes enough for 6 slices of thick sourdough or other rustic bread, grilled, or toasted in the oven at 200°C/gas 6 for about 5 minutes.

Broad beans, black olives and tomato

When fresh broad beans are not available, frozen ones are fine. Like peas, they are protected in their skins so the freezing process perfectly preserves them.

1 You need around 500g of freshly podded or frozen broad beans. **2** Cook them in boiling salted water for 2 minutes, then drain under cold running water and preferably slip off the skins, unless the beans are very small and young. **3** Put into a bowl, add around 2 tablespoons of good black olives (minus their stones) and lightly crush them together. **4** Mix in 2 large diced tomatoes and a tablespoon of white wine vinegar. **5** Scatter in some fresh mint leaves and a tablespoon of extra virgin olive oil, and toss everything lightly together. **6** Taste, season as you like with sea salt and freshly ground black pepper, and spoon some of the mixture on to each slice of toasted bread.

Broad beans, black truffle and shallot dressing

Again, frozen broad beans are perfectly good for this. If you prefer, you can substitute shaved pecorino for the black truffle.

1 You need around 500g of freshly podded or frozen broad beans. **2** Cook them in boiling salted water for 2 minutes, then drain under cold running water and preferably slip off the skins, unless the beans are very small and young. **3** Put into a bowl and crush lightly. **4** Make a dressing with ½ tablespoon of white wine vinegar, a tablespoon of extra virgin olive oil and a teaspoon of chopped shallot, add to the beans and toss lightly. **5** Season to taste with sea salt and freshly ground black pepper and a few shavings of black truffle. **6** Spoon some of the mixture on to each slice of toasted bread and finish with some more shavings of black truffle.

Quail and chicken liver

This takes a bit of work, but it is a lovely thing to do.

1 You need 3 whole quails, cleaned. **2** Heat some olive oil in a large pan, then season the quails inside and out and put them into the pan, skin side down. Sauté until the skin turns golden, then turn over and add half a glass (35ml) of white wine. **3** Bubble up to evaporate the alcohol, then pour in around 200ml of good chicken stock (you need enough to cover the quail) and simmer for 30 minutes, until the meat flakes away from the leg bones. **4** Take off the heat and keep on one side. **5** When cool enough to touch, flake the meat and put into a bowl, reserving the cooking juices. **6** In another pan heat some more olive oil and put in a finely chopped shallot, a finely chopped celery stalk, a few leaves of sage and 400g chicken livers. **7** Season with sea salt and freshly ground black pepper and cook until the livers begin to caramelise. **8** Add 2 tablespoons of brandy and 2 tablespoons of Marsala. **9** Take off the heat, finely chop the livers and mix into the quail meat, with the rest of the contents of the pan. If the mixture is too dry, add a little of the reserved cooking juices from the quail. **10** Season and mix in some fresh thyme leaves. **11** Spoon some of the warm mixture on to each slice of toasted bread.

Beef tartare

I really, really love this. It is best to chop the steak straight from the fridge with a sharp knife, preferably on a marble surface to keep the meat really cold, rather than put it into a food processor, which warms it up and changes the texture and taste. You can even put the chopping board into the freezer first, if you like.

1 Rinse 2 salted anchovies very well and dry them on kitchen paper. **2** Beginning at the tail, run your thumb gently along the backbone of each anchovy, which will allow you to pull it out and separate the fish into 2 fillets. **3** Chop them finely. **4** Rinse and drain a teaspoon of capers in vinegar. **5** Put 300g of very finely chopped lean steak into a bowl, add a teaspoon of finely chopped shallots, the anchovies and capers, mix together and season to taste with sea salt and freshly ground black pepper. **6** Mix in 2 tablespoons of extra virgin olive oil and spoon some of the tartare on to each slice of toasted bread.

Mozzarella and ham calzoncini

We all fell in love with these little pasties when we were on holiday in Sicily, where they have them in all the bakeries, and when it comes to aperitivo time at around midday, plates of them would appear on the counters of the local bars. They are a very simple thing, but it is the umami action of good mozzarella and ham, which is a combination that is repeated time and time again in Italian cuisine, that makes them so hard to resist – though you could also make them with some blanched, chopped spinach and fresh ricotta. So we started making them at home. I would make the dough in the morning and put it into the fridge, then we would go out for the day, and finish the *calzoncini* off and bake them when we came back. The only thing Margherita couldn't have was the egg wash which I like to put over the top to give a good colour and sheen, so hers would be made separately. I remember her and Jack standing by the oven, asking all the time, 'Are they ready yet, are they ready yet...?'

Don't roll the dough too thinly; that is quite important, as it is not meant to be thin and crisp. Part of the experience is the way the moisture from the mozzarella helps the dough to stay soft inside. And keep the *calzoncini* quite small: two bites and they should be gone.

1 Mix all the dough ingredients in a bowl, then turn it out and knead it for around 10 minutes, until firm but elastic. 2 Cover with a clean tea towel and leave for an hour until it rises by about a third. 3 Divide the dough into 20 pieces and roll each one into a ball. 4 Space them out on a large plate or tray and cover as before. 5 Leave for another hour, until doubled in size. 6 With a rolling pin, flatten each ball into a disc about 5mm thick. 7 Divide the ham and mozzarella equally between the discs. 8 Fold over the dough to make a little pasty and pinch the edges together. 9 Preheat the oven to 220°C/gas 7. 10 Line a baking tray with baking paper and lay the calzoncini on top. 11 Brush the top of each one with beaten egg and sprinkle with sesame seeds. 12 Bake in the preheated oven for 10–12 minutes, until golden.

Makes around 20 calzoncini

For the dough:

strong white flour 500g

strutto (lard) or butter 60g

fresh yeast 15g

milk 130ml

water 110ml

sea salt 15g

egg 1

sugar 1 teaspoon

For the filling:

slices of cooked ham 5, chopped

mozzarella 400g, diced

For the topping:

egg 1, beaten

sesame seeds 1 tablespoon

Fennel taralli

These are the answer to artificially aggressively flavoured crisps. You can buy bags of *taralli* – little ring-shaped snacks, similar in texture to grissini – in supermarkets all over Italy, but I find the commercial ones a little greasy and heavy, whereas when you make them yourself with fresh yeast and good extra virgin olive oil they can be incredible. Originally they were very much a speciality of the south. If you go to Puglia, Basilicata, Calabria or Campania, the people will all tell you they invented them, and their own variation, with chilli, black pepper or local wine added into the dough, is the true one. Some versions are sweet, instead of salty.

I like them just flavoured simply with fennel seeds. We used to make them with Margherita and Jack when they were small, as kids love them, and it is a very, very easy dough for them to make a game of helping to roll and shape.

1 In a bowl mix the yeast with 50ml of water at room temperature. **2** Mix in all the rest of the ingredients, together with 160ml of hot water, and work for around 10 minutes into a smooth dough. **3** Cover with a clean tea towel and leave to rest for 20 minutes. **4** Preheat the oven to 180°C/gas 4. **5** Roll out the dough 1cm thick then cut into long strips about 2cm wide. **6** Now cut each strip crossways into strips 5mm wide and roll each one with your fingertips until it is about 4cm long. **7** Form each of these into a ring, pushing the ends together to seal. **8** You will need to bake the taralli in batches. Line two baking trays with baking paper, and arrange the rings on top, spacing them about 1cm apart. **9** Leave for 30 minutes, until they have risen a little. **10** Bake in the preheated oven for about 8–10 minutes, or until the taralli have turned a deep golden, then switch off the oven and open the door slightly to allow air to circulate and dry them out a little, before removing and leaving to cool. **11** Now you can store the taralli in an airtight container or jar for about a month.

Makes around 80 taralli

fresh yeast 15g
00 flour 250g
semolina flour 250g
extra virgin olive oil 100ml
sea salt 15g
fennel seeds 1 teaspoon (optional)

Grana Padano puffs

These are full of natural umami, and whenever we make them for parties, they disappear the moment they are put out. So if you have a big family I suggest you double or treble the quantities!

I first made them to serve with San Daniele ham when I was filming in Friuli Venezia Giulia in the northeast of Italy, where these famous hams are cured with sea salt to special specifications demanded by their Protected Designation of Origin status.

I was always fascinated by the history of the hams, which are so recognisable because they have their feet still attached. The Celtic people, and after them the Romans, began salting and curing pork in the particular cold, dry microclimate created by the meeting of the breezes from the Alps and the Adriatic Sea which allowed them to be cured with a low amount of salt. For 700 years San Daniele came under the protection of the patriarch of the ancient Roman town of Aquileia, who allowed it to become a free market, and so the hams were traded with Venice and the royal courts of Europe, especially Vienna. Pigs and hams were so important to the town and the region that people used them like cheque books, to pay their debts.

These were the hams that were always served at our family restaurant, La Cinzianella, in Corgeno. My uncle Alfio used to leave in the morning to drive to San Daniele to fill the car up with 25–30 hams and bring them back to the restaurant. Me and my brother, Roberto, would sit on the wall waiting for him, for hours sometimes, then as soon as he arrived we had to carry in the hams and my grandad would be waiting to hang them up from the rafters. I was entranced by the shapes of the hams, with their feet, and the pervasive meaty, salty smell, intensified by the warmth of the car, which is so elemental, it is almost the smell of life.

I used to watch the old chef Michele, and after he died, the new chef Silvano, taking out the bone so that you had a beautiful, compact piece of ham, ready to go on to the slicing machine. On Saturdays when we would do banquets and wedding receptions, as soon as the people arrived and were having their drinks, the chefs would begin the slicing, very, very thinly. Every inch of the kitchen would be covered in huge plates of ham, ready for the waiters to take out one by one.

It seems to me now that those days at La Cinzianella were just the best. The preparing and slicing of the hams was an incredible operation, I loved it so much, and by the time I was considered old enough to prepare the hams myself, I already knew exactly how to do it, because I had watched the chefs a hundred times.

So I wanted to make something special to put out with the ham. I liked the idea of some little *zeppole*, fritters made with potato dough, to serve with the ham, and since ham and cheese is so much a part of the Italian flavour palate, I put some Grana Padano, aged for 24 months, in the dough, and also a little piece inside so that would melt when the puffs of dough were fried. Grana Padano has a slightly sweeter, more 'cheesy', less salty and distinctive flavour than Parmigiano Reggiano, and also it melts at a lower temperature, so it is the perfect cheese for this.

As a variation, you could also push a piece of anchovy, sun-dried tomato or olive paste into the dough before deep-frying.

Grana Padano puffs (see picture on previous page)

1 Cook the whole potatoes, still in their skins, in salted boiling water until tender. **2** Drain, peel off the skins and put the flesh into a bowl. **3** Crush with a fork, then weigh it – you need 370g, to equal the quantity of the flour. **4** Return the potato to the bowl and while still warm, add the flour, yeast, salt and grated Grano Padano, together with 600ml of warm water, and mix until you have a soft dough. **5** Cover the bowl with clingfilm and leave at room temperature for about an hour, until almost doubled in size. **6** Heat some vegetable oil to 180°C in a deep-fryer (alternatively, heat the oil in a large pan, no more than a third full – if you don't have a kitchen thermometer, drop a little flour into the oil and it will sizzle very gently). **7** Take a teaspoon of dough at a time, push a piece of Grana Padano into the centre and smooth the dough over the top. **8** In batches, slide them into the hot oil for about 2 minutes, until the dough puffs up and turns golden, then lift out with a slotted spoon and drain on kitchen paper.

Makes around 30–40 puffs

potatoes 450g
00 flour 370g
fresh yeast 20g
sea salt 20g
Grana Padano 150g, grated, plus around 120g, broken roughly into 5mm cubes
vegetable or seed oil for deep-frying

To serve:
slices of San Daniele or Parma ham (optional)

Rice crisps
x 4

For me it was always important that my children snacked on something healthy, but at the same time, I didn't want to say, 'No, you can never have things that are fried,' because of course fried things can be so delicious. So these are a great compromise. Yes, they are deep-fried, but they are made with risotto that you have cooked yourself, so you know exactly what has been put into it, and that you have allowed to 'overcook' until the grains of rice are no longer al dente but soft. Then it is blended into a creamy paste, spread over a sheet of baking paper until it dries out and can be broken into pieces, and deep-fried until these puff up into crazy shapes that always surprise people, and that kids love. Margherita, of course, couldn't eat these when she was younger, as until recently she was allergic to rice, but we would make similar ones for her with polenta (see page 263).

Rice crisps were featured in the first picture I ever put on Instagram, after we created some spectacular-looking ones at Locanda for a reception being held for the Accademia Italiana Della Cucina. We made three kinds of risotto, in the colours of the Italian flag: a classic white one; a red one, flavoured with tomato; and a green one, flavoured with spinach (the recipes are overleaf). When the creamy mixture was spread really, really thinly over the baking paper, hairline cracks naturally appeared as it hardened, so when it was broken up and deep-fried the pieces puffed up like big veined leaves.

We use water instead of chicken stock to make the risotto, as stock has its own colour and flavour and is quite opaque, whereas clear water allows the rice to colour more dramatically.

As well as the white, red and green crisps, we have added another recipe using black rice, which makes crisps that are a deep aubergine colour. You can make all the crisps any size you want – though the bigger they are, the more fun they look – and add some additional flavours, if you like. A little chilli would be incredible added to the plain white version before blending it, or you could add a few strands of saffron when you are cooking the onions, which would give an additional touch of flavour and a beautiful golden colour.

White

1 Melt a knob of butter in a small heavy-based pan, add half an onion, finely chopped, and season lightly with sea salt and freshly ground black pepper. **2** Cook gently until the onion is soft and translucent, but don't let it brown, otherwise it will have a burnt flavour and spoil the white appearance of the finished crisps. **3** Turn up the heat to medium, and add 50g of carnaroli or arborio rice. Stir around until the grains are well coated in the butter and onion, but don't take on any colour. **4** Once the grains are heated through, start to add around 1.2 litres of boiling water, a ladleful at a time – just enough to cover the rice – and stir with a wooden spoon until almost all the water has been absorbed, before adding the next ladleful. The grains of rice will start to swell and release their starch into the pan, as you carry on stirring and adding the water. Normally when you make a risotto, after about 17–18 minutes it will have reached the perfect point when the rice is plump and tender but each grain has a slight firmness at the centre. But for this recipe you need to carry on stirring and adding more water if necessary for another 5–7 minutes, making sure that the rice doesn't stick to the bottom of the pan, as it will become very starchy.

5 When the grains of rice are completely soft, take off the heat and spoon the rice into a blender. **6** Blend until creamy, then add a tablespoon of grated Parmesan and blend again quickly – just for 30 seconds. If necessary add another 2 tablespoons of boiling water. **7** Taste and season, then with a spatula spread the mixture very thinly (about 2mm) over a sheet of baking paper. **8** Leave for 12–14 hours, until completely dry and crispy, then break into pieces of whatever size you like. **9** Heat some vegetable or seed oil to 180°C in a deep-fryer (alternatively, heat the oil in a large pan, no more than a third full – if you don't have a kitchen thermometer, drop a little flour into the oil and it will sizzle very gently). **10** Put in the pieces of dried risotto, a few at a time, for just about 10 seconds: they will puff up to around double their size. **11** Lift out with a slotted spoon and drain on kitchen paper.

Red

1 Make the risotto as above, but once it is blended, stir in a tablespoon of good tomato purée and continue with the recipe.

Green

The flavour of the spinach really comes through well in this variation.

1 Blanch about 2 tablespoons of chopped spinach for a minute in salted boiling water, then drain and with your hands squeeze out as much water as possible.
2 Make the risotto as opposite, then stir in the squeezed spinach before blending and continue with the recipe.

Black

Black rice is an ancient grain, high in antioxidants, iron and fibre. It has a nutty flavour and when it is cooked it is actually not black, but a deep purple colour.

1 Make the risotto as opposite, but with 50g of black rice, and cook it for 40 minutes, stirring and adding more water as necessary, then continue with the recipe.

Carta di musica with bottarga and lemon

Think of *carta di musica* as a fantastic substitute for unhealthy nibbles, to put out before a meal with a glass of wine. You can buy these paper-thin, crisp rounds of bread in Italian delis and online, and I always like to have a packet or two in the cupboard. They are so called because of their resemblance to the old parchment used for music manuscripts, and were originally Sardinian shepherds' food – in Sardinia they're known as *pane carasau*. Although the sheets of bread are so thin, amazingly they don't break easily, so they could be carried by the shepherds out into the fields.

Carta di musica is made by forming the dough into small balls which are rolled out into thin rounds, then they are baked on one side, turned over and baked on the other side, so they puff up. Then each round is split horizontally into two thin sheets. The process always reminds me of the way that you split thick slices of bread for melba toast, which nobody seems to make any more, but that I used to love when I was at the Savoy. I remember there was one guy in the kitchen who did nothing but make the melba toast all day.

The *carta di musica* are beautiful quickly toasted in the oven, then stacked up and put out with some shavings of bottarga and a little lemon juice and extra virgin olive oil. Or, if you don't have bottarga, they are just as good with some chopped ripe tomato.

In Sardinia they also layer up the sheets of bread with tomatoes and cheese and put them into the oven – this is called *pane guttiau* in Sardinian dialect. Or there is another version done with eggs, which they call *pane frattau*. That is one of my favourite things: I put a sheet of *carta di musica* into a deep plate, ladle a little hot stock over the top, so that the bread collapses, crack an egg on it, put in another piece of *carta di musica*, and pour some more really hot stock on top. By the time the stock begins to cool down, the egg will be cooked but the yolk will still be runny, then you can grate some pecorino over the top and finish off with some black pepper.

1 Preheat the oven to 180°C/gas 4. **2** Put the sheets of carta di musica one on top of each other on a baking tray and put them into the oven for about 1 minute, until they turn golden in patches.
3 Remove from the oven and spread out the breads on a large board.
4 Grate the bottarga over the top and finish with a squeeze of lemon juice and a little olive oil and black pepper.

Serves 6

carta di musica about 12

bottarga 120g

lemon 1, halved

extra virgin olive oil 2 tablespoons

freshly ground black pepper

Cherry tomato focaccia

In its simplest form this Tuscan-style focaccia is one of the most forgiving of bread doughs, thanks to the olive oil, which makes it more pliable. Also, it doesn't involve any kneading; instead you use a technique of stretching, dimpling and folding the dough, then dimpling it some more, which is what gives it its light airiness and its characteristic look. So, although I understand that not so many people have the time or patience to bake bread a lot at home, this is a great one to make every so often, to cut or tear into pieces and have by itself for a mid-morning or afternoon snack, or to put out with prosciutto, mozzarella and salads.

The cherry tomatoes need to be really sweet, so it is the perfect bread to make in the summer with tomatoes that have been sitting in a bowl in the kitchen and have become a bit over-blown and almost semi-dried, as their flavour will have intensified as the moisture has been drawn out of them. Incidentally, tomatoes that have reached this stage of maturity are also brilliant simply sautéd in olive oil with a little garlic for a pasta sauce (see page 146) – add some chilli if you like. If you don't have any cherry tomatoes, but have larger ones that are really ripe, just cut them into six and use them instead.

This is quite a large bread, so if you have a small oven, it is better to divide the dough in half and bake two.

As with any baking, calmness is the key. Don't rush, and if possible make the dough when the kitchen is still warm from cooking, as it will behave better than in a cold environment.

(see pictures on next page)

1 Halve the cherry tomatoes and lay them in a shallow dish.
2 Scatter over a pinch of sea salt and the basil leaves, then sprinkle 2 tablespoons of the olive oil on top and leave to marinate for 2 hours at room temperature. **3** In a bowl mix the flour, salt, yeast and the rest of the olive oil with 440ml of warm water and work it until you have a quite soft dough. **4** Cover the bowl with a clean tea towel and leave to rest for 30 minutes.

5 Now turn out the dough on to a clean work surface, and with your hands vertically over the dough, press down with your fingertips to dimple and stretch it out sideways at the same time, into a rough rectangle about 40cm x 30cm and around 1cm thick. It is this technique that creates air pockets and gives the softness and lightness that is typical of focaccia. **6** Next, fold the top third of the dough towards you as far as the centre, and dimple it lightly again with your fingertips. Then fold the bottom third over the top, again as far as the centre, and dimple it again. Now you need to turn the dough through 90 degrees and repeat the process from the beginning again. **7** Leave to rest for 30 minutes, then repeat the whole dimpling, stretching and folding process described above, all over again. **8** Leave to rest for a further 30 minutes. **9** Preheat the oven to 220°C/gas 7.

10 Transfer the dough to a baking tray. **11** One by one, lift out the tomatoes from their marinade (but reserve this), and push them, cut side up, into the dough. **12** Discard the basil, but if bits of the leaves go into the dough with the tomatoes, this is fine. **13** Brush the tomato marinade over the top and leave to rest (uncovered) for another 30 minutes. **14** Just before you put the focaccia into the oven, sprinkle a pinch of sea salt over the top, then bake for around 16 minutes, until the bread has puffed up and is golden. **15** Take out of the oven and transfer to a wire rack to cool down. **16** Leave it for around 30 minutes to rest before eating, to give it a chance to dry out a little, so that if you press it it will bounce back, and be crispy on top.

Makes 1 large or 2 smaller focaccia

ripe cherry tomatoes 1kg

fine sea salt 20g, plus a little coarse sea salt for the tomatoes

fresh basil leaves about 10

extra virgin olive oil 4 tablespoons

00 flour or strong bread flour 750g

fresh yeast 22g

Ligurian focaccia

This is a fantastic bread which I really wanted to include, as the flavour and structure is quite different from the spongy Tuscan-style focaccia on pages 128-9 that everyone knows. If you can ever categorise people, there is something about the Ligurian character that is quite tight and tenacious, that shows in the powerful, essential flavours of their food, stripped back, with nothing unnecessary added, and this bread, with its fantastic crispy, salty crust, is typical. Unlike Tuscan focaccia, it is a bread to eat warm and in Liguria you see people queuing outside the bakeries just waiting for it to come out of the oven.

I still remember the moment I ate it for the first time on holiday when I was growing up. A friend of mine used to come skiing with our family each winter, and so in return his family invited me one summer to the house they had taken in the seaside town of Sestri Levante. The only time I had been away from home before was on holiday camps with my brother, and so everything was new and different, and on the first morning, the mother said, 'Let's go and have breakfast.' The custom was to go first to the bakery to buy the focaccia, which the baker would cut into rectangles and wrap up for you, and then take the bread with you to the nearest bar, where you ordered bowls of coffee latte. It was perfectly acceptable to bring your bread with you. I like that attitude: one person bakes, another makes coffee, everyone is happy. I remember we sat at tables outside in the sunshine, drinking the coffee and eating this bread that was familiar, yet like nothing I had tasted before, and I was blown away by the combination of salt and crunch and milky coffee. It was such a revelation because at home for breakfast I had only ever had bread with jams. I wolfed everything down and the family were watching me and laughing. 'Do you like it?' 'I love it!' 'Then you can have some more...' I was totally hooked.

Because of the heat and the humidity, bread-making around the Ligurian coast can be a nightmare, which is why many of the traditional specialities feature dried doughs, such as galettes, and this bread relies less on the formation of the dough and more on the stretching, to give it the elasticity it needs. Because it is thinner it doesn't last as well as a Tuscan focaccia, so you need to bake it and eat it quickly, but that is never usually a problem!

(see picture on previous page)

1 Mix all the focaccia ingredients in a bowl with 230ml of water – make sure this is at room temperature, not cold – until everything comes together in a dough, then cover the bowl with clingfilm and leave to rest for 30 minutes. **2** Brush a roasting tin with a little extra virgin olive oil.

3 Turn out the dough on to a clean work surface and flatten it out, stretching and dimpling it with your fingertips until it is just under 1cm thick. **4** Cover with clingfilm and leave for 30 minutes. **5** For the brine, mix the sea salt and extra virgin olive oil together with 2 tablespoons of water, so that the salt dissolves. **6** Remove the clingfilm and dimple and stretch the dough again as before. Don't worry if it is a little thinner or thicker in places. **7** Brush with the brine, making sure you cover all the dough, including the dimpled areas, as once in the oven the olive oil will do the job of creating the contrast of crispiness outside and softness inside that is the characteristic of the bread. **8** Leave the dough to rest for 30 minutes, uncovered.

9 Meanwhile, preheat the oven to 220°C/gas 7. **10** Lift the focaccia into the prepared tin and bake in the preheated oven for 13–15 minutes, until the top is golden and crispy, and preferably eat while still warm.

Makes 1 large focaccia, about 30cm x 40cm

00 flour 250g

strong bread flour 250g

extra virgin olive oil 50ml

fine sea salt 15g

fresh yeast 18g

For the salamoia (brine):

coarse sea salt 1 tablespoon

extra virgin olive oil 80ml

Raisin bread

This is *pan tramvai,* which is a famous raisin bread in Lombardy, and was such an important thing in my family and in our region. My grandad especially was so attached to it, as I guess for the older people who had been through the war this was the only sweet thing they had, because there was no sugar available. Yes, there was some fruit grown, but I am sure that the jamminess of the raisins was something special that delivered that rush of euphoria sugariness brings when you have been starved of it. It is something that we cannot really understand now, when the level of sugar that our society consumes has spiralled out of control, but the people of my grandparents' generation always spoke of *pan tramvai* with a smile on their faces.

And it does the same for me now. I remember one evening I came home late from a long day's filming and joined Plaxy and her mother, who were having dinner at a little restaurant in north London. All I wanted was some bread and cheese and when the waiter brought the bread basket it had little raisin rolls in it, which made me so happy.

It is said that the name *pan tramvai* comes from the fact that it was made in a bakery beside the tram stop in Monza where, at the turn of the century, commuters took the slow tram into Milan to work. So when they bought their tickets they would also buy some *pan tramvai* to eat for breakfast. I used to do a similar thing when I stayed behind at school for sports practice a couple of times a week and I would buy a little piece of it to eat on the bus on the way home.

I like it for breakfast, too, and it is good toasted. Jack used to love it done like *pain perdu,* passed through some beaten egg and milk and pan-fried in butter. And I especially love it with some cheese and fruit – maybe pears or grapes – or celery, and a little red onion or green tomato chutney. My absolute favourite combination is with fresh ricotta, pecorino or caciocavallo cheese and honey. You could also use the bread to make a rich bread and butter pudding. The celebrated Milanese chef Gualtiero Marchesi used to make a famous dessert of raisin bread and butter pudding and custard.

The quality of the raisins you use is important. I used to find beautiful ones for this bread in Sicily, where they are crazy about dried fruit. Sometimes you can find bags of different-coloured ones (organic preferably), which make the bread look incredible.

Once made, you can keep the bread in the freezer if you like.

1 Mix the flour, salt, yeast and olive oil in a large bowl and gradually mix in 290ml of warm water until you have a dough consistency, then add the raisins and work them in. **2** Roughly shape the dough into a long loaf, place on a baking tray and cover with a clean tea towel. **3** Leave to rest for 1 hour and 40 minutes. It will rise, but since this is quite a heavy bread full of fruit, it won't double in size as other doughs do. **4** Preheat the oven to 220°C/gas 7. **5** Bake in the preheated oven for 30 minutes, until it is golden on top and sounds hollow when you tap the base.

Makes 1 loaf

strong bread flour	500g
fine sea salt	1 tablespoon
fresh yeast	20g
extra virgin olive oil	2 tablespoons
raisins	500g

As long as I can open
my kitchen cupboard
and see a packet of
spaghetti, a bag of
risotto rice and some
00 flour, I know I will
always have the basis
of a meal.

Pasta, rice and pizza

Orecchiette with tomato and salted ricotta

Orecchiette, or 'little ears', are such a typical Puglian thing, a very ergonomically shaped pasta that was being made by hand long before the invention of machines to pass the pasta through dyes, or moulds, to shape them and then dry them. When orecchiette are made by hand, the pasta dough is rolled out into thin cylinders, which are cut into little pieces and then pressed and curled into an ear shape in one deft movement. Because the strands of protein are aligned first one way, in the rolling, and then in the opposite way in the pressing and stretching, this builds a great strength into the pasta, so that it is capable of holding any sauce, especially an oily, tomato-ey one. I like to imagine that this ancient instinctive technology in the home kitchen was how we learned to build and strengthen materials for later industries, like car manufacturing – Italians always claim that everything began with pasta!

When we are on holiday in Puglia we buy our orecchiette fresh from the *pastificio*, where they are made with quite a rough texture so that they really cling well to whatever sauce you make, but the place that is most famous for handmade orecchiette is Bari Vecchia, the old medieval part of Bari, which has its own community, completely different to that of the newer part of the town around the port. In certain courtyards bounded by tall houses with balconies, the women, often with their mothers, grandmothers and small children, set up tables outside their doors each morning with their homemade pasta dough, ready to make the orecchiette. There is a whole social life built around the cutting and shaping, as these women sit and chat with their neighbours, sometimes singing, and their dexterity is incredible. They work so fast, not even looking at what they are doing, and within minutes their tables are full of the little ears. At about 12 o'clock the townspeople arrive on their scooters, bicycles, in their cars or on foot to buy the orecchiette, take them home, maybe to their mothers, to cook them for lunch, and then they go back to work or their daily life.

Orecchiette are brilliant with sauces made with olive oil and vegetables, such as *cime di rapa* (turnip tops) with chilli and garlic, anchovies too, if you like. If you are using dried orecchiette, look for ones that have been shaped using a traditional bronze die. This gives them a slightly rough edge so that they hold on to the sauce better than a more shiny pasta cast with a teflon die.

I also love orecchiette with tomato sauce and salted ricotta. Ricotta (which means re-cooked) is a very southern Italian thing, made using the ancient idea of bringing the whey left over from cheese-making up to a high temperature in a pot, then skimming off the creamy sweet-tasting proteins that rise to the surface and draining them in rush baskets. The story goes that it was first made accidentally by a shepherd who left a pot of whey on the fire after cooking up a rudimentary cheese in a field with his flock.

Once drained, the fresh ricotta (*fresca*) is sold in tubs, but because it is quite delicate and cannot be kept, some of it is also salted, pressed and matured, so that it becomes semi-hard and can be sold by the piece, for grating over pasta or salads. You can keep this *ricotta salata* (salted ricotta) in the fridge for years, and it will never go off, because it has been both cooked, and salted and matured. Even if it grows a little mould, just scrape this off and the cheese will still be good.

I love salted ricotta, but it is a bit of an underdog in the cheese world, outshone by Parmesan and Grana Padano. It has a different, almost fluffier, consistency than those cheeses that makes it exceptionally elegant and velvety in the mouth. It is typically grated over pasta Norma, the Sicilian dish made with aubergines, and I like it grated over a spinach salad, or in a sandwich with honey: that combination of sweet and salty is delicious.

Orecchiette with tomato and salted ricotta

1 Heat half the olive oil in a sauté pan, add the onion and garlic and cook gently until the onion is soft and translucent, taking care not to burn the garlic. **2** Put in the tomatoes, cover with a lid, simmer for 5 minutes, checking and adding a little water if the mixture dries out, then season to taste. **3** Cook the orecchiette in a pan of boiling salted water for about 8–10 minutes (or according to the packet instructions) until just al dente, then drain, reserving a little of the cooking water. **4** Toss the orecchiette in the tomato sauce, with half a ladleful of the cooking water and about a quarter of the ricotta, let it rest for a minute, so that the pasta can really suck in the sauce, then toss it again. **5** Add the basil, drizzle with the extra virgin olive oil, and scatter the rest of the grated ricotta over the top.

Serves 6

olive oil 2 tablespoons	
onion 1 small, chopped	
garlic 1 clove, finely chopped	
ripe cherry tomatoes 500g, quartered	
sea salt and freshly ground black pepper	
fresh or dried orecchiette 500g	
salted ricotta 200g, grated	
fresh basil leaves 5	
extra virgin olive oil 2 tablespoons	

Tomato sauce
x 4

For me a plate of spaghetti with tomatoes and basil can be as good as any dish in the world. I would pay as much to eat it as lobster, or risotto with white truffle. For Italians it is one of our emotional food triggers. There is something so comforting and welcoming about it, and when it is done perfectly it completely captures the beauty of simplicity.

People think a tomato is a tomato, always in the supermarket, to use all year round. No. In the height of summer, of course, it is fantastic to make a fresh sauce for pasta or pizza with brilliant tomatoes that are still on the vine, but in the winter it is much better to use tinned tomatoes, or bottled passata, or roast your tomatoes in the oven so that you concentrate the flavour.

The big trend towards buying passata hopefully means that people are turning more to making their own sauces instead of buying ready-made ones that often contain high levels of sugar and salt. There are some brilliant passatas available, but the only way to discover a good one is to heat up a few in a pan and smell and taste them. I want acidity and that true, almost sharp hit of tomato flavour.

A tin of tomatoes can also be brilliant, because the best canners pick the tomatoes and process them at the perfect moment of ripeness but, again, check the ingredients to see if sugar or salt has been added. Sometimes you do need to add a touch of sugar if the tomatoes are tasting too acidic, but that should be your choice. In Italy people will argue family to family over the best brand of tinned tomatoes. I would say it is worth paying more for the big San Marzano plum tomatoes grown in the volcanic soil around Mount Vesuvius, because they have thin skins and a high ratio of flesh to water and fewer seeds. Always read the labels, though, because simple mathematics tells me that to satisfy market demand the whole of Italy must be covered in tomatoes, with no room for people! There is always the possibility that tomatoes may be grown or processed in other countries then returned to Italy to be bottled or canned and receive their Italian passport!

Each recipe overleaf will serve 6 with pasta.

With fresh tomatoes

1 Cut 1kg of ripe cherry tomatoes into quarters.
2 Heat 4 tablespoons of olive oil in a large pan. **3** Add 2 finely chopped cloves of garlic and the tomatoes.
4 Scatter in around 5 leaves of fresh basil, season with sea salt and freshly ground black pepper, cover with a lid and cook very gently for 10 minutes, stirring every 3–4 minutes. The sauce is ready when the tomatoes have released their juices.

Passata

This is the pure tomato pulp that all our grandmothers and grandfathers made. You can buy very good passata in bottles, but there is a certain satisfaction in making your own when there are plenty of brilliant tomatoes in the summer.

1 Put 1kg of ripe tomatoes into a large pan with 100ml of water. Halved or quartered San Marzano tomatoes are good, because they have a high ratio of flesh to seeds and are low in water, as are cherry tomatoes which can be left whole. **2** Put the lid on and bring to the boil very gently. **3** Cook for 5 minutes, or until the tomatoes are soft. **4** Put through a food mill to remove the skin and seeds, leaving just the pure tomato pulp.
5 Transfer to a sterilised bottle or bottles (if you like you can add a couple of fresh basil leaves to each bottle), then stand these in a pan lined with a tea towel. Use another tea towel to put between the bottles to stop them clinking, if necessary. **6** Fill with cold water, put the lid on the pan and bring to the boil, turn down to a simmer for 30 minutes, then remove, cool and store. Provided it is sealed and unopened it should keep for up to a year. When ready to use, just add the passata to sautéd onion and garlic and cook according to your recipe.

With chopped, tinned tomatoes

1 Heat 3 tablespoons of olive oil in a pan, add a finely chopped onion and a finely chopped clove of garlic and cook gently until the onion is soft and translucent, taking care not to burn the garlic. **2** Add 2 x 400g tins of good chopped tomatoes, then rinse out the tin with fresh water and add to the pan. **3** Season with sea salt and freshly ground black pepper. **4** Bring to the boil, then turn down the heat and cook very gently for 30 minutes. **5** Tear about 5 fresh basil leaves roughly and scatter them into the sauce.

With roast tomato

Once roasted these could be put around a fish you are baking in the oven, halved and tossed through pasta with basil or other herbs; or they can be added to salad leaves with a little fresh ricotta on top, drizzled with olive oil and finished with some freshly ground black pepper – Plaxy loves them like that. You could also crush them onto crostini, maybe with some anchovies or olives on top.

1 Preheat the oven to 180°C/gas 4. **2** Spread out 1kg of whole, ripe cherry tomatoes on a baking tray, season with sea salt and freshly ground black pepper and put into the oven for 10 minutes, until the tomato skins start to split and some of the juice seeps out. **3** Remove from the oven and sprinkle with a little dried oregano.

To make a roasted tomato passata, put the tomatoes through a food mill as in the recipe opposite.

Calamarata with samphire, monkfish, chilli and lemon

Calamarata are so called because they are shaped like rings of squid, and they are one of the latest dried pastas to develop a fashionable image, along with paccheri and mezzi paccheri (see page 150) – you could also use mezzi paccheri for this recipe. I really enjoy cooking with calamarata because they are perfect for absorbing and holding a light but quite velvety wine-based sauce like the one here. This is quite an unusual dish because the pasta is cooked in water that has been infused with lemon peel. Monkfish can be very rich, and the delicate lemony accent that is taken up by the calamarata counteracts that and works really well.

The combination of flavours has its roots in a pasta I made on a break in Wales with Plaxy and Jack. We went to the market and bought a whole monkfish – mainly because Jack was so fascinated by its big ugly head – as well as some local samphire and lemons, the big, very yellow ripe ones you get in spring and summer. Jack wanted to have the monkfish fillets wrapped in bacon and roasted in the oven, the way we often did it at home, but after I had prepared the fish I was left with lots of small pieces of cheek and tail which I didn't want to waste. So I decided to make a pasta sauce, caramelising the pieces of fish in olive oil and then adding the samphire and a little of the zest and juice of the lemons, and that is how it started. I liked the flavours so much that we began to work on it in the kitchen at Locanda, refining it and tweaking it into the recipe here, and now if we put it on the menu, people go crazy for it.

1 With a peeler remove the peel from the lemons in large strips.
2 Pour 5 litres of water into a large pan, add the lemon peel and bring to just under a simmer (if you have a kitchen thermometer this will be 80–90°C). **3** Take off the heat, cover with a lid and leave to infuse for 2 hours. **4** Pass the infused water through a fine sieve into a large bowl (you want to remove the pieces of lemon peel, as if they find their way into the finished sauce they will be bitter), then return the water to the pan and bring to the boil, adding some salt.

5 Put in the pasta and cook for about 12 minutes (or 3 minutes less than the instructions on the packet). **6** Meanwhile, put one of the cloves of garlic on a chopping board and crush it into a paste with the back of a large knife. **7** Put the parsley on top and chop finely, so that the garlic and parsley combine and release their flavours into each other. **8** Finely chop the remaining garlic cloves. **9** Heat a little olive oil in a large sauté pan, and add the garlic and the chilli. **10** Cook gently for 2 minutes, taking care not to burn the garlic. **11** Add the monkfish and cook for another 2 minutes, pour in the wine and let it bubble up to evaporate the alcohol, then stir in a ladleful of the cooking water from the pasta. **12** Drain the pasta, reserving the rest of the water. **13** Add the pasta to the sauce, with enough of the cooking water to almost cover it. **14** Add the samphire and capers and let the liquid reduce by half, until it coats the pasta. **15** Finish with the parsley and garlic and olive oil and spoon into a warmed serving dish. If you like, finish with a squeeze of lemon juice.

Serves 6

unwaxed lemons 4, preferably Italian

sea salt and freshly ground black pepper

calamarata pasta or mezzi paccheri 500g (see page 150)

garlic 3 cloves

fresh flat-leaf parsley a small bunch

extra virgin olive oil a little

mild red chilli 1, finely chopped

monkfish fillets 300g, cut into small pieces

white wine ½ glass (35ml)

samphire 100g, cleaned

salted capers 1 teaspoon, rinsed and dried

Mezzi paccheri with gurnard, olives and tomato

One of my favourite restaurant experiences was in Naples, in a place on the cliff overlooking the Bay of Marechiaro, where the local lawyers and doctors go to eat. We ordered gurnard, which came out, whole, in tomato sauce in a big dish, then big tubes of cooked paccheri pasta arrived which the waiter mixed into the sauce, then covered the plate with two or three cloths and went away. He came back again after about five minutes, opened up the cloths, turned the pasta in the sauce a few times and then served it, just taking pieces of gurnard fillet off the bone as he did so, and it was incredible. Some of the paccheri had kept their tubular shape, others were flattened and closed around the sauce, so there was a mixture of textures. Of course we ate it by the sea, which always helps to lift the senses, but it was such a simple, brilliant idea that when I was on holiday in Puglia I did a similar thing with a whole grouper.

The great thing about paccheri is that you leave it in the sauce soaking up the flavours for quite a few minutes and don't worry about it, because it is so sturdy it is almost impossible to overcook it. If you manage to do it, let me know, because you must be a genius.

There is a story that the pasta was invented as an ingenious vehicle for smuggling cloves of garlic across the border between Italy and Prussia (Austria) in the early seventeenth century. The authorities had banned the import of the big, juicy cloves grown in southern Italy, which the people in Prussia preferred to the smaller ones produced by their own farmers, which were not as good, and their livelihoods were under threat. So in Sicily they began making these big dried pasta tubes that were big enough to hide around four cloves of Italian garlic inside when they were sold across the border.

Until not so long ago paccheri was still a very local pasta, only known and eaten close to the area of production in Sicily and Campania, and if you mentioned the name to an Italian, they would not know what you were talking about, but now it is much more familiar, and you can easily find it in packets in supermarkets and delis in the UK. It is an interesting style of pasta because when the tubes are cut in the factory they are done on the bias, so one side is slightly different to the other, and when they are cooked – which takes longer than most pastas – they collapse and become a bit flat, trapping the sauce inside. They are delicious in this kind of silky sauce made with fish. Personally, though, I find them a little too big, not quite elegant enough. I see people being given a plate of them and wondering, 'What shall I do? Cut them? Eat them half at a time? In one go?' So for this pasta, I like to use mezzi paccheri, which are the same diameter, but half the length. They still release plenty of starch into the sauce so that it coats the tubes perfectly, and the tubes are still big enough to allow the pieces of fish, olives and almonds to get caught inside, but they are easier to negotiate.

Gurnard is a relatively cheap fish whose head and bones make a good stock. Even if you don't want to go to the bother of chopping up vegetables, just simmering the bones in water for 20 minutes will give you so much flavour, but if you want to skip this stage altogether, you can use water instead.

Try to use good black olives, which are not really black, but deep purpley-brown depending on the variety, and not the artificial black ones that come sliced in tins and that you see on cheap pizzas. Crush the whole olives lightly with their stones in, as that extra touch of bitterness that comes from the stones is very important. And please, buy almonds with their skins on, as the skin contains so much goodness, and blanched ones are often treated, to keep them white. If you really can't bear the texture of the skins, you can wet your hands after you have roasted the almonds in the oven, and just dampen the nuts, then wrap them in a clean tea towel and rub them until the skins come off.

Mezzi paccheri with gurnard, olives and tomato

1 Preheat the oven to 180°C/gas 4. **2** Lay the almonds on a baking tray and put them into the oven for about 7 minutes, moving the tray around and giving it a shake occasionally so that the nuts become golden all over. **3** Remove the tray from the oven and allow the nuts to cool, then chop quite finely, but not too evenly, so that you have different textures in the finished sauce.

4 To make the stock, heat a little olive oil in a large pan, add the onion, carrot and celery with the herbs and cook gently until the onion is soft and translucent. **5** Add the fish heads (minus the eyes) and bones and continue to cook for a couple of minutes. **6** Add the tomato purée and stir all together for 2 minutes. **7** Finally, add 1.5 litres of water and bring to the boil, then turn down to a simmer for 15 minutes. **8** Pass through a fine sieve and keep to one side.

9 Put one of the garlic cloves on a chopping board and crush into a paste with the back of a large knife. **10** Put a handful of parsley leaves on top and chop finely, so that the garlic and parsley combine and release their flavours into each other. **11** Cook the pasta in plenty of boiling salted water for about 12 minutes (or 3 minutes less than the time given on the packet instructions). **12** Meanwhile, remove the skin from the fillets of gurnard, and cut into chunks. **13** Chop the other garlic clove finely.

14 To make the sauce, heat the olive oil in a pan, add the garlic and chilli and cook gently for about a minute, taking care not to burn the garlic. **15** Add the pieces of fish, season, and cook for 3 minutes, stirring, until the fish becomes flaky and tries to stick to the bottom of the pan. **16** Add the wine and let it bubble up until the alcohol evaporates completely, then add half the reserved stock and the olives.

17 Drain the pasta and add to the pan of fish and sauce for 3 minutes, until the pasta has taken up some of the sauce, which should retain its silky consistency. If it starts to become dry, add a little more stock – don't worry that the pasta might overcook. It won't. **18** Add the tomatoes and the parsley and garlic. **19** Continue to stir, adding the extra virgin olive oil. Taste and adjust the seasoning if necessary. **20** Spoon into a warmed serving dish and scatter with the toasted, chopped almonds.

Serves 6

almonds 2 tablespoons, skin on

garlic 2 cloves, finely chopped

fresh flat-leaf parsley a small bunch (keep the stems for the stock)

mezzi paccheri or other short tubular pasta such as calamarata 500g

sea salt and freshly ground black pepper

gurnard 3 medium, filleted, but heads and bones reserved

olive oil a little

mild red chilli 1, chopped

white wine ½ glass (35ml)

black olives, preferably Taggiasche 2 tablespoons, crushed with the stones in, then stones removed

cherry tomatoes 10, halved

extra virgin olive oil 2 tablespoons

For the stock:

olive oil a little

onion 1, finely chopped

carrot 1, finely chopped

celery 1 stalk, finely chopped

bay leaf 1

stems from the parsley (see above)

heads and bones from the gurnard (see above)

tomato purée 1 tablespoon

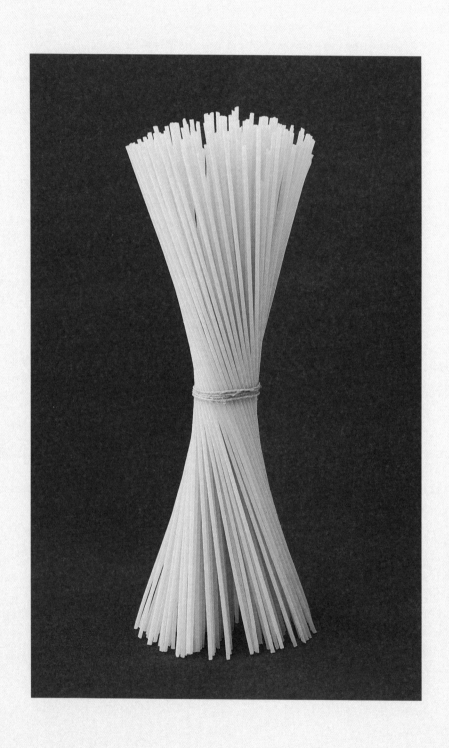

4 a.m. Spaghetti
x 4

These are the classic store-cupboard-and-fridge pastas that every Italian teenager knows; the ones you make almost on autopilot when you come home after a night out with your friends, and go straight to the cupboard or the fridge, desperate for some carbohydrates. Later on, they are the pastas you make when you arrive home late from holiday and your kids are calling for food. Then when they get older and are going out with their own friends, the cycle repeats itself when they fall back on the same recipes when they come home in the early hours, albeit with their own twist, according to what they like, or can lay their hands on. I have often opened the fridge in the morning to find a little bowl of spaghetti left over after Margherita or Jack have been cooking in the early hours, and they always taste amazing.

But these spaghettis are not just convenient, quick and easy dishes; they can also be seductively brilliant, a perfect example of how a dish can be so much more than a sum of its parts.

Let's not forget that the quality of the spaghetti, especially in these very simple pastas, is important. It is not just a vehicle for a sauce. A fantastic dried pasta carries a very smooth, rounded, wheaty, almost beery-yeasty aroma and flavour. So many things can make a difference: the variety of wheat, stone grinding, the control of the temperature in the drying rooms, as well as the perforated mould, or dye, that is used to extrude the pasta through. The temperature of different metals and surfaces can make a difference to the taste and texture. I like a little roughness on the surface of a spaghetti that has been extruded through a bronze, rather than teflon, die. The small family company Verrigni, who make outstanding dried pasta in Abruzzo, have even perfected a gold die which makes the pasta smoother than a bronze one, but also increases its absorption and intensifies the flavour.

The pillars of Italian pasta – a few notes

Aglio, olio e peperoncino (garlic, oil and chilli)

Spaghetti with oil, garlic and chilli has become famous after it featured in the sexiest scene of the film *Chef*, in which John Favreau plays a guy who loses his restaurant job after a bad review, so he buys a truck and goes off on the road selling Cuban food. In a late-night scene he makes this unctuous, oily, garlicky spaghetti for the character of Molly, his former restaurant manager, played by Scarlett Johansson, winding it around a big toasting fork and handing it to her in a little bowl, then watching her as she is totally seduced by the flavours. It is a moment of genius. The way she watches him making the spaghetti, and then he watches her eat it, it is so much more powerful than if he had just given her a plate of expensive oysters and caviar.

This is a very simple but luscious spaghetti, with just the three ingredients talking to you, so be forceful with them, as the oil, which needs to be a big fruity one, must be rich and busy with the flavours of garlic and chilli. Don't be scared to add three, four or five sliced cloves of garlic per person, as it must have a real presence, and don't be shy with the chilli either; I must admit I like some real heat, so I would use a Scotch bonnet, seeds and all, but how hot you make it is up to you. Chillies in red and green are nice, too, if you have them.

The real trick to this is to start with just a little extra virgin olive oil in a sauté pan and put in your sliced garlic while the oil is still cold. Raise the temperature slowly and just before the garlic starts to fry, pull the pan off the heat, add a little more cold oil, then put it back on the heat. Keep doing this several times, adding a little more of the cold oil each time, so that you keep the temperature down and the garlic is not frying, but just infusing the maximum amount of its flavour into the oil before you put in the chilli. If you were to start with the chilli, especially if the oil is very hot, you would smother the aroma and flavour of the garlic.

Cacio e pepe (cheese and pepper)

If you have some pecorino in your fridge, then the late-night spaghetti to make is *cacio e pepe*, literally cheese and pepper. First of all the age of the cheese – pecorino – is very important. You need a very young one. A bit like some people, mature cheeses will have been on their own for a long time, developing their characters so they don't necessarily welcome new flavours, whereas a young pecorino is still impressionable and likes to mix and melt. Pecorino comes from all over Italy, but pecorino romano is the best one to use for this, as it is less strong and salty than the Sicilian or Sardinian pecorinos. If possible use a microplane to grate it, which is much better than a regular standing grater – though if you only have one of these go for the smallest side. Don't push the cheese, just caress it against the microplane or grater so that it falls like snow, as if you press and condense it it will become grainy.

Because pepper is the only other ingredient, it also becomes very important. It isn't there just for heat, but for real flavour, too. When I was cooking at Le Laurent restaurant in Paris, I first came across single-estate peppercorns, which were very unusual and expensive at that time and came in little jars especially for a complicated carpaccio of scallops and black truffle. Peppercorns are grown on a vine. When they are picked young they are green and when they are allowed to mature on the vine and then sun-dried they become black. White peppercorns are black ones which are soaked to remove the outer dark casing.

Usually when you buy black peppercorns they are a generic mix of different varieties of peppercorns from various countries, but if you use a single variety from a particular region from India to Indonesia or Malaysia, it can make a great difference, and you can discover amazing aromas and flavours from citrus to nutmeg when you crush them. I prefer not to do this in a mill, but with a meat hammer, the end of a rolling pin, or the back of big knife, so that the peppercorns crack into irregular pieces, and I do this just before I use them, so that the aroma and flavour is really fresh.

Some people will swear that to make a good *cacio e pepe* you need to toast the peppercorns a little in the dry pan over a low heat, like an Indian spice. I am not convinced of that. Yes, the peppercorns will release some beautiful oil and aroma, but that is exactly the problem, I don't want these to be released yet, I want them to stay in there and then release into the oil and water. But maybe I am wrong. It is a matter of opinion, so you choose. Personally I just warm the crushed pepper in a little olive oil and then add a ladleful of the cooking water from the pasta and stir it around so that the water becomes quite 'scummy', which is what you want, before you add the drained spaghetti.

Carbonara

The first thing I have to say about spaghetti carbonara is that cream should never appear in the ingredients. By all means make a pasta sauce with cream, cream cheese or milk, add mushrooms if you like, and it will be delicious, but just don't call it carbonara.

Although I can say for certain how to make it properly, I cannot say for certain how, where or why it was first made. Nobody really knows, except that *alla carbonara* means 'in the style of coal workers'. So maybe the pasta got its name because the crushed pepper in it resembles coal, or it may have been made originally by the workers who chopped wood in the mountains to make charcoal. And why should a dish of cured pork and eggs originate in Rome? Do they have more eggs or pigs there? No.

For me the most sensible explanation is that eggs were surely cooked with pasta and pieces of ham in homes all over Italy, but the big explosion in popularity happened when there was rationing during the Second World War and for a long while afterwards. At the same time the areas of vegetable production around Rome suffered in the bombings. Italy was still a society that relied on local agriculture, so there was a big domino effect and people in the city would have had very little food. They would walk sometimes for 10 or 20 kilometres to pick wild herbs and bring them home to sell in the market to make a little money to sustain themselves, something that is so difficult to imagine for those of us who have never faced anything like that. Then the Americans arrived, big and strong and healthy, in contrast to the gaunt, hungry people of Rome that you see in old photographs, and they brought bacon, and powdered eggs to share around, which would have been perfect to mix with water for spaghetti.

The true cured pork to use for carbonara is guanciale, which comes from the cheek, and has less fat than pancetta. Don't cut it too finely or regularly, as you want a nice chunk to bite into every now and then amid the silkiness of the egg. And the cheese should again be a young pecorino romano, not Parmesan. Some people add the eggs and cheese to the pan of cured pork and spaghetti, but it is easy to underestimate the heat of the pan, and the danger is always that the eggs will scramble. So I prefer to mix the eggs and cheese in a warm bowl and then tip in the hot spaghetti, which will cook the eggs but keep their silkiness.

It may seem like heresy, but actually tubular pasta like rigatoni or penne is also very good with carbonara sauce.

Tuna, tomato and olives

Finally, I have added this very simple store-cupboard spaghetti – though the sauce also works well with penne, or another tubular pasta. In Italy you can buy expensive glass jars of tuna belly, like the Spanish *ventresca*, but I don't feel that you want rarified, delicate tuna for this. It is one to make with the kind of canned tuna that most of us have in the cupboard. I prefer to buy tuna in spring water rather than oil, as often the oil is quite cheap and will spoil the flavour.

Each recipe overleaf makes enough for 6

With the exception of the *cacio e pepe*, allow 1 litre of water to every 100g of pasta, so that the spaghetti has plenty of room to move about, and add a teaspoon of salt per litre of water. The quantity of pasta we seem to have settled on these days is around 70g per person, especially if the pasta is being eaten as a starter, but I would say anywhere between 70g and 100g is about right for these spaghettis, depending on how hungry you are and if you are eating anything else to follow.

Aglio, olio e peperoncino (garlic, oil and chilli)

1 Start cooking 500g of spaghetti in plenty of boiling salted water, and slice your chilli (around a tablespoonful, or more if you prefer) and around 4 cloves of garlic about a millimetre thick. **2** You need around 200ml of good extra virgin olive oil, but start with a little of it, cold, in the pan. Put in your garlic, then keep taking the pan off the heat and adding a little more cold oil, then returning it to the heat so that you don't burn the garlic (see page 156). **3** Once all the oil is in, you can let the garlic begin to take on a little bit of colour and put in your chopped chilli. Let it cook very briefly, stirring it into the garlic, then pull the pan from the heat and stir in a couple of spoonfuls of the cooking water from the pasta – take care, as it may spit. **4** When the pasta is cooked but still al dente, lift it out and drain it, but keep back the cooking water. **5** Toss the pasta really well through the oil, garlic and chilli, adding a little more cooking water from the pasta if it is too dry, as you want the garlicky hot oil to really cling to the spaghetti, and serve straight away. If you like, you can toss through a tablespoon of chopped fresh parsley and finish with some grated Parmesan or pecorino.

Cacio e pepe (cheese and pepper)

1 Grate around 5 tablespoons of young pecorino romano, or more to taste. **2** Start boiling your water for the pasta. For this recipe, because it contains only cheese and pepper, the water becomes an important ingredient that binds these ingredients to the pasta, therefore you want as much starch from the pasta in it as possible. So only use 3 litres of water for 500g of pasta. This also means using less salt (a teaspoon) and stirring the pasta around in the water becomes pivotal, so that it doesn't stick to itself. So give it your full attention: it is only for 5–6 minutes, until al dente. **3** Once the spaghetti is in, crush around 2 teaspoons of black peppercorns in a sauté pan using a steak hammer or the end of a rolling pin – it is easier to do this in the pan than on your work surface, otherwise the peppercorns will fly everywhere – add a little olive oil, stir in a ladleful of the cooking water from the pasta and bubble up. **4** Now drain your spaghetti (reserving the cooking water), add it to the sauté pan along with the grated cheese and toss everything together really well – the spaghetti will carry on cooking a little more, and so will release more starch into the pan. **5** Add a little more of the cooking water from the pasta as necessary so that it combines with the melting cheese to give a creamy consistency.

Carbonara

1 Chop about 10 slices of guanciale or pancetta. **2** Begin to cook 500g of spaghetti in plenty of boiling salted water. In a sauté pan, heat a knob of butter, then put in the guanciale or pancetta and fry until golden and crispy. **3** Take off the heat, and lift out the guanciale or pancetta to a warm plate, so that it stays crunchy. **4** Put about a teaspoonful of black peppercorns into the pan and crush with a meat hammer or the end of a rolling pin, then add a couple of spoonfuls of the cooking water from the pasta and stir it around to take up all the bits of guanciale or pancetta which may have stuck to the bottom of the pan. **5** Beat 5 egg yolks and a whole egg in a warm bowl with 3 tablespoons of grated young pecorino romano. **6** One minute before the spaghetti is ready, start to mix in a ladleful of the cooking water at a time to the eggs and cheese until they become creamy. **7** Drain the pasta (but reserve the cooking water) and toss it in the pan of pepper, together with the reserved guanciale or pancetta. **8** Add a little more cooking water if the pasta seems too dry, then transfer it to the bowl of eggs and cheese and toss well, until coated in the silky mixture. The heat of the spaghetti will cook the eggs without scrambling them. **9** Add more black pepper, if you like.

Tuna, tomato and olives

You could substitute sardines for the tuna if you prefer. You can use green olives, but good black ones such as Taggiasche are better. Buy them with the stone in – olives without stones are not allowed in our house – and crush them, so that the bitterness from the stone is released into the flesh, before pitting them. If you have some capers in a jar, you could rinse and drain them and add those too. I suggest finishing the pasta with some chopped fresh mint leaves, but you could use parsley, oregano or marjoram, whichever you have, but no cheese with fish, please.

1 Heat 4 tablespoons of extra virgin olive oil in a sauté pan, add 2 finely chopped cloves of garlic, a teaspoon of chopped chilli and a tin of chopped tomatoes, bring to the boil, then turn down to a simmer for 10 minutes. **2** Cook 500g of spaghetti in plenty of boiling salted water. **3** Just before it is ready, add 2 x 200g tins of drained tuna and a small handful of good black olives to the tomato sauce, then taste and season with sea salt and freshly ground black pepper. **4** Drain the pasta, reserving the cooking water, and toss with the sauce and a spoonful of the cooking water. **5** Scatter some chopped fresh mint leaves over the top, and serve.

Vincisgrassi

Baked pastas play an important part in our family eating, and *vincisgrassi*, a speciality of the Marche region, known for its cured hams, butter and wild mushrooms, is one of the simplest, which kids seem to love. I would make up batches of it to keep in the freezer for Margherita, but with peas instead of mushrooms. The most extravagant recipes, such as the legendary *vincisgrassi* my friend Franco Taruschio used to make at the Walnut Tree Inn near Abergavenny, are a big celebration of only fresh porcini (ceps) in season, but a mixture of wild mushrooms is fine. You can include some fresh porcini if you like when the mushrooms appear in the autumn (sometimes you can also find frozen porcini, which are excellent).

The pasta is supposed to have been created in 1799 for a dinner to honour Prince Windischgratz, who was commander of the Austrian forces in Ancona in the Marche region during the Napoleonic wars. However, as always in Italian culinary history, there is a dispute over the story, since an earlier, similar dish called *princisgras* was mentioned in a book called *Il Cuoco Maceratese* ('The Cook of Macerata' – Macerata being a province of the Marche region), published in 1871 by Antonio Nebbia, which looked at the fashionable foods of the day.

1 In a large pan, bring the chicken stock to the boil, add the dried mushrooms, then take off the heat straight away and leave to infuse for 1 hour. 2 For the béchamel, bring the milk to the boil in a pan, and season. 3 In a separate pan, melt the butter, whisk in the flour and cook gently for 3 minutes over a low heat. 4 Gradually whisk in the milk and continue to whisk over a low heat for 2 minutes, until you have a thick sauce. 5 Take off the heat and keep warm.

6 Lift the dried mushrooms from the stock (but retain this) and chop them finely. 7 Melt the butter in a large pan, add the garlic, Parma ham and chopped dried mushrooms and cook for 2 minutes, taking care not to burn the garlic. 8 Put in the sliced mixed mushrooms and cook for another 3 minutes to release their liquid, then add the white wine, bubble up to evaporate the alcohol, and finally pour in the reserved chicken stock. 9 Bring to the boil, then stir in three-quarters of the béchamel sauce and take off the heat. Keep the rest of the béchamel to one side. 10 Preheat the oven to 180°C/gas 4.

11 In a large ovenproof dish, ladle some of the béchamel, mushroom and ham mixture over the base and cover with four of the pasta sheets, overlapping them a little if necessary so that there are no gaps. 12 Ladle in another layer of the béchamel mixture, followed by about 2 tablespoons of grated Parmesan. 13 Repeat the whole process of layering twice more, but use the reserved, plain béchamel for the final layer, and top with plenty of Parmesan. 14 Put into the preheated oven for 20–25 minutes, until golden and crispy on top.

Serves 6

good chicken stock 400ml
dried porcini mushrooms 30g
butter 50g
garlic 2 cloves, lightly crushed
sliced Parma ham 150g, chopped
mixed wild mushrooms 400g, sliced
white wine 1 glass (70ml)
dried lasagne 20 sheets
Parmesan around 200g, grated

For the béchamel:
milk 2 litres
sea salt and freshly ground black pepper
butter 140g
plain flour 140g

Ravioli
x 4

My favourite ravioli, since childhood, is one of the simplest, filled with spinach and ricotta. Sometimes we ate out as a family at a restaurant on Lake Maggiore, where we would always have these to start, tossed in butter and sage, with a fish like perch to follow, or *lavarello spaccato*, the local lake fish, filleted and fried, with a piece of lemon, and chips for us kids as a special treat.

There are an infinite number of shapes and fillings for ravioli. The only thing I would say is that if you have never made them before, it might take a few times to feel really confident, but what is the worst thing that can happen? You throw away your dough, get some dried pasta from the cupboard and use the filling that you have made with that instead. Don't make your ravioli too early, make them no more than an hour before you want to serve them, as the humidity from the filling can soften the pasta, causing the ravioli to break when you cook them.

I like to make quite a firm pasta dough, as if it is too soft and elastic it will stretch when it is rolled through the pasta machine, but then pull back when you are making your ravioli and become too thick. So if you are mixing the dough by hand and your hands aren't hurting by the time you have finished, you are not doing it properly.

Make it the day before you need it, wrap it in clingfilm and put it into the fridge overnight, then when you come to put it through the pasta machine it will be beautiful.

Ravioli
x 4

The base recipe (makes enough for 36 ravioli)

Sift 500g of 00 flour into a bowl, then turn it out in a mound on to a clean work surface. Make a well in the centre and sprinkle in a pinch of fine sea salt, then crack in 2 large eggs and 2 egg yolks. Break the eggs with your fingertips and gradually work in the flour in a circular movement until you have a dough which will come together in a ball.

Alternatively, if you want to use a food processor, sift the flour into the bowl, add the salt, and then, with the motor running slowly, add the egg yolks followed by the whole eggs. Stop and turn out the dough as soon as it comes together. Now you have to knead it by pushing it with the heel of your hand, then pulling and folding it back over itself, and repeating this over again for as long as it takes for the dough to feel quite springy. Wrap it in clingfilm and leave it to rest in the fridge for at least an hour, but preferably overnight.

To roll the pasta

First flatten the dough into a square about 1cm thick with a rolling pin. Make sure it will go through your pasta machine easily. There is no precise number of times to put the pasta through the machine, you will need to feel your way with it, but roughly speaking, follow these steps: Feed the pasta through the machine on its biggest setting, then put it through again on the next setting down. Repeat this two or three times, then fold the pasta back on itself, in half, put the machine back on to its first setting and put the pasta through three or four more times, taking the setting down one each time, until the pasta starts to become silky.

Now cut the pasta in half and cover one half with a damp cloth. Fold the other half in three: fold one end in and the other end over the top, so that it is square-shaped. Turn it through 90 degrees, then put it through the machine on the first setting again – by changing direction you build strength and elasticity throughout the pasta. Repeat a few times, taking it down a setting each time. Finally, fold the pasta back on itself, in half, one last time.

Put the machine back on to the first setting and run the pasta through again, taking it all the way down through the settings until it is about 1.5mm thick, shiny and see-through.

Make your ravioli from this strip of pasta, before rolling the next one. Mark the centre point of the strip, then brush one half with beaten egg. Place small mounds of your pasta filling (about a teaspoonful) on top – two abreast and with about 3–4cm between them. Fold the other half of the pasta over the top, matching the sides, and press down gently around each mound of filling.

Using a fluted round cutter 1cm bigger than the filling, cut out each raviolo, then gently press out any air around the filling. Repeat with the other strip of pasta.

To cook

Bring a large pan of water to the boil. Put in the ravioli and cook for 3–4 minutes.

Pesto: perfect with ravioli

In the recipes overleaf I suggest serving pesto with the potato ravioli, but pesto is brilliant with almost any pasta. It makes perfect sense to me that the home of pesto is Liguria, because this is a region where the cooking is very essential and stripped back to powerful flavours. When I was on holiday as a kid in Sestri Levante with one of my friends and his family – the same occasion that I first discovered the local crispy, salted focaccia (page 132) – at the end of a day on the beach, swimming and playing games, we would be ravenous, so we used to go to a little restaurant in the middle of town run by 'the two aunties'. There was no menu, they just made two or three simple dishes, including an open lasagne built up of sheets of thin, fresh egg pasta, beautiful bright green pesto and grated cheese, which they brought out and you cut up and shared. It was so delicious, and we were always so hungry we would order another and another, until we were all full.

At the same restaurant I tasted minestrone with a spoonful of pesto in it for the first time, which was one of those moments that I have never forgotten. This soup that I had known all my life suddenly exploded with flavour.

I prefer to make pesto in the traditional way with a pestle and mortar, which is a very satisfying thing to do at home. I know it seems easier to whiz all the ingredients, apart from the oil, in a food processor or blender, then incorporate the oil at the end, but you cannot underestimate the way the friction of the blade can warm up the ingredients and sweat the oil from the nuts, which changes the structure and flavour of the pesto. Whereas if you crush and grind the ingredients in stages it breaks them down in a very different way. If you were to give two people identical ingredients and ask one to pound them and the other to whiz them you would end up with two very different pestos. If you really want to use a food processor, the best thing is to put the bowl in the fridge so that it is really cold before you start.

In Liguria they have special mortars with four handles which allow you to turn them as you work, and a wooden pestle and stone mortar is considered the perfect combination. I also like the big, heavy granite mortars that you find in Thai shops.

Remember that a good pesto should taste of garlic, but not only garlic, of basil, but not only basil, and of pine nuts and pecorino, but not only of pine nuts and pecorino. It is all about balance, and of course that balance is a matter of individual taste. Even in Liguria, which is divided in two with Genoa in the middle, people will fall out over the best way to make it. In Ponente, north of Genoa, they tend to like it more cheesy and nutty, so it is whiter, while in Levante, to the south, it is more green and herby, but as always the detail changes from town to town, village to village and family to family.

Personally, if I have brilliant basil, I like to let it do the talking. Each year we have five or six boxes of very special small sweet leaves from the village of Pra in Liguria in early summer, but it doesn't last long. The smaller the basil leaves the better, because they are less fibrous, and so the pesto will be more creamy. If I have only bigger leaves, then I might step up the other ingredients. The only thing I wouldn't add too much of is garlic, and some people put no garlic in at all.

A trick I do if I am at home and making a simple pasta with pesto is to chop up a potato into small pieces and put it into the pan of boiling salted water about 10 minutes before I put in the pasta. Then, when the pasta is drained and tossed with the pesto, the potato breaks up and the starch in it helps the pesto to cling on to the pasta.

To make the pesto

Preheat the oven to 180°C/gas 4. Spread 2 tablespoons of pine kernels over a baking tray and put into the oven for about 5 minutes, moving the tray around once or twice until the nuts are golden. Smash 2 cloves of garlic with a small pinch of salt, using a pestle and mortar, then add the toasted pine kernels and crush them into the garlic and salt, but don't overwork them. Add 250g of fresh basil leaves, preferably small, sweet, fragrant ones, a few at a time, again working them in as quickly as you can. Now work in 2 tablespoons of grated pecorino or Parmesan, and finally add 300ml of good olive oil, preferably a Ligurian one, until you have a bright green paste. The quicker you are, the brighter and fresher the colour and flavour.

A little shellfish stock

If you are making a prawn ravioli like the one overleaf, and want to add an extra layer of flavour, buy prawns with the shell on and make a little stock from the heads and tails. Sauté them in a little olive oil with some chopped celery, carrots and onions, a bay leaf and a few fresh parsley leaves, add a tablespoon of tomato purée and enough water to cover, bring to the boil, then turn down to a simmer for 15 minutes. Pass through a fine sieve and use instead of water, to cook the ravioli.

The recipes overleaf make enough for 6.

Ricotta and spinach

1 Blanch 600g of spinach in boiling salted water for 1 minute, drain under cold running water, then with your hands squeeze out all the excess water. **2** Finely chop the spinach and put into a bowl, add 600g of fresh ricotta, an egg, a handful of grated Parmesan and a pinch of nutmeg, and mix well. **3** Taste, season with sea salt and freshly ground black pepper, then use a teaspoon to fill the ravioli and cook them as on page 164. **4** In the meantime melt 150g of butter in a pan and put in a few fresh sage leaves. As soon as the butter starts to bubble, add a ladleful of the boiling water from the pasta pan to create an emulsion. **5** Lift the ravioli out with a slotted spoon and transfer to the pan of butter and sage for a couple of minutes, then serve, sprinkled with grated Parmesan.

Cod and chickpeas

1 Either cook 300g of dried chickpeas as on page 206 (but cut the vegetables into larger dice) or heat up good jarred or tinned ones. **2** Take out three-quarters of the chickpeas and blend, adding some extra virgin olive oil and a little of their liquid until you have a smooth purée. Keep the rest to one side. **3** Put a clove of garlic on a chopping board and crush it into a paste with the back of a large knife. **4** Put a handful of fresh parsley leaves on top and chop finely, so that the garlic and parsley combine. **5** Heat some olive oil in a large pan, put in 2 finely chopped shallots, 2 finely chopped stalks of celery and 3 anchovy fillets. **6** Cook gently until the shallot is soft and translucent, then add 600g of chopped, skinless cod fillets. **7** Cook, stirring, for 5 minutes, until the fish is cooked. **8** Season with sea salt and freshly ground black pepper and put into a bowl. **9** Cool, then mix with 3 tablespoons of olive oil and a teaspoon of chopped fresh parsley leaves. **10** Fill the ravioli with the cod mixture and cook as on page 164. Lift out with a slotted spoon and transfer to the pan of chickpeas and vegetables. **11** Sprinkle with the parsley and garlic and serve on the purée. **12** Finish with a little grated lemon zest.

Potato, green beans and pesto

People sometimes say, 'Potato in pasta?' but once they taste these ravioli they love them.

1 Boil 15 new potatoes in their skins until just tender, then drain. **2** As soon as they are cool enough to handle, peel them and put 12 of them into a blender with 120g of butter and 40g of grated Parmesan and blend until smooth. **3** Cover with clingfilm and keep on one side until cool. **4** Cut the remaining potatoes into cubes. **5** Cook around 30 green beans in boiling salted water until just tender, then drain under cold water and split each one in half lengthways. Keep to one side. **6** Make the pesto as on page 165. **7** Fill the ravioli with the potato mixture and cook as on page 164. **8** Just before they are ready, put the reserved green beans and cubed potatoes into the same pan to warm them up. **9** Meanwhile, put the pesto into a pan with a little warm water, just to loosen it. **10** Lift out the ravioli, beans and cubes of potato with a slotted spoon and drain them. **11** To serve, spoon some of the pesto into warmed bowls, add the ravioli, green beans and cubed potatoes and sprinkle with some more grated Parmesan.

Prawn and courgette

1 Heat some olive oil in a large pan, put in a finely chopped clove of garlic, cook for a minute, then add around 900g of large, peeled raw prawns and sauté for a couple more minutes. **2** Season with sea salt and freshly ground black pepper and add half a glass (35ml) of white wine. **3** Bubble up to evaporate the alcohol, then add 2 tablespoons of tomato passata, take off the heat and put into a blender. **4** Blend to a purée, then leave to cool down. **5** Put 2 cloves of garlic on a chopping board and crush them into a paste with the back of a large knife. **6** Put a large handful of fresh parsley leaves on top and chop finely, so that the garlic and parsley combine and release their flavours into each other. **7** Mix half of this into the prawn purée, reserving the rest. **8** Fill the ravioli with the prawn mixture. **9** Dice 2 courgettes. **10** Heat some olive oil in a large pan, put in a lightly crushed clove of garlic, then add the courgettes and sauté until soft and lightly golden, taking care not to burn the garlic. **11** Add half a glass (35ml) of white wine and 10 quartered cherry tomatoes. **12** Cook the ravioli as on page 164. **13** Lift out with a slotted spoon and transfer to the pan of courgettes and tomatoes, with a couple of ladlefuls of the cooking water. **14** Toss through, adding the rest of the parsley and garlic.

Pappardelle with rabbit, olive and thyme rag

When my brother and I were growing up we were taught a great respect for the rabbits my grandad kept. During the war, when there was so little food, it was rabbits that kept his generation going, and I don't remember anyone around us who didn't raise them for the table.

About once a month grandad would kill one of the rabbits, and he taught us that the whole process was perfectly natural. When I was quite small, I remember saying, 'But grandad, the rabbit looks really scared,' and he told me, 'Yes, maybe a little bit, but he knows he is doing something really good for us.' So we accepted very early on that the rabbits had a good life, they were fed well, and then it was their turn to make their contribution to feed the family. We had a connection with the animals and a sense of responsibility for them that I feel is lost when meat is sold in packs in supermarkets.

Rabbit is a very good, healthy white meat which has so much less impact on the environment than, say, beef cattle, but choose ones that have been raised organically or in high-welfare systems. Avoid intensively farmed rabbit, most which is produced outside the UK, as the rabbits are likely to have led a miserable life in cramped cages.

You can buy really good fresh and dried pappardelle, but if you want to make fresh pasta yourself, there is a recipe on page 164. At Locanda when we make pappardelle, we press some thyme leaves into it, which makes it look very beautiful. We make sure we use the leaves only, as the stalks can make little holes in the dough when it is put through the pasta machine. We wash them, but don't dry them completely, as if they are a little damp you can spread them over the dough just before it is folded and is put through the machine for the final time, and they will cling. As the pasta goes through the machine the leaves are pressed inside and the green colours show through. Cut the sheets of pasta into ribbons, 2cm wide.

1 For the ragù, heat the olive oil in a large pan. 2 Season the pieces of rabbit, put them into the pan and colour them on all sides until golden, then lift them out on to a warm plate and keep to one side. 3 Put the onion into the pan and cook gently until soft and translucent. Add the wine and bubble up to evaporate the alcohol, scraping the bits from the base of the pan, then sprinkle in 1 teaspoon of the thyme leaves and put back the rabbit. 4 Cover with the chicken stock and simmer for 1 hour. 5 Take out the rabbit and strip the meat from the bones. 6 Bubble up the liquid in the pan until it reaches a sauce consistency, then add back the rabbit meat and put in the olives. 7 Cook the pappardelle in plenty of boiling salted water for 3–4 minutes for fresh pasta (if using dried pasta check the timing on the packet), drain, reserving the cooking water, and toss with the ragù, adding a little of the cooking water along with the butter, Parmesan and the rest of the thyme.

Serves 6

olive oil 2 tablespoons

sea salt and freshly ground black pepper

large rabbit 1, cut into 12 pieces

white onion 1, chopped

white wine 100ml

fresh thyme leaves 2 teaspoons

good chicken stock 2 litres

black olives, preferably Taggiasche 60g, lightly crushed with the stones still in, then stones removed

fresh or dried pappardelle 600–800g

butter 50g

grated Parmesan 3 tablespoons

Pappardelle with hare, red wine and chocolate ragù

The first trigger for this recipe was the typical northern Italian way of braising hare *(lepre) in salmi* – red wine – especially in the wine-producing regions of Piemonte. My uncles would go out shooting and if they brought back a hare, my grandmother would wash it in water and vinegar, check for any fragments of shot and then put it into a wine marinade, with onions and celery, juniper berries and rosemary, which would soften out the flavour of the strong-tasting meat, as well as tenderise it.

I have suggested a bottle of Chianti, but any full-bodied red wine with some complexity, depth and strength would be good, such as a Sangiovese, or an Argentinian Malbec. Then the important thing is to let the hare cook very slowly. Hares are very muscular – think how fast they run. So if you cook the meat too fast it will become dry.

When my grandmother made hare *in salmi* we would grate Parmesan over the top, but much as I love Parmesan on most pasta, I felt that in this case it was a distraction from the hare. It wasn't adding anything, and I was looking for something to really heighten the experience of the dish when I happened to watch our chocolate supplier, Willie Harcourt-Cooze, grate 100 per cent Venezuelan cacao over avocado and eggs using the same action as for Parmesan, and something just clicked in my mind. So I tried adding some of the cacao into the sauce and some over the hare at the last minute. As some of the cacao fell on to the hot serving plates, there was an explosion of chocolate aroma that you breathed in before you even tasted the pasta, to which the cacao added richness rather than flavour, and I thought it worked beautifully. 10g may not seem like much to put in, but remember we are talking about chocolate at its most essential and complex, before sugar has been added, so any more would make the sauce bitter.

Ask your butcher to cut the hare for you, following the joints and taking care not to smash the bones, in case they splinter.

(see picture on next page)

1 Put the hare into a bowl. **2** Mix together all the ingredients for the marinade and pour over the meat. **3** Leave in the fridge for 24 hours. **4** When you are ready to cook, remove the hare from the marinade and keep the meat to one side. **5** Bring the marinade to the boil in a pan, then take off the heat and pass through a fine sieve into a bowl. **6** Have the flour ready in a shallow bowl. **7** Pat the pieces of hare dry and season them, then dust in the flour.

8 Heat the olive oil in a large pan, add the hare and colour on all sides, taking care not to burn the flour, then lift out and keep to one side. **9** Put the chopped vegetables and juniper berry paste into the pan and cook gently until soft. **10** Pour in the Chianti and bubble up to evaporate the alcohol and reduce the liquid by half.

11 Put back the hare and add the reserved marinade and enough chicken stock to cover. **12** Add the bay leaf and rosemary. **13** Bring to the boil, then turn down the heat, stir in half the cacao and simmer for 2 hours. **14** Take out the hare and strip the meat from the bones. Keep to one side. **15** Reduce the cooking liquid to a sauce consistency, then return the hare meat to the pan.

16 Cook the pappardelle in plenty of boiling salted water for about 3–4 minutes (if using dried pasta check the timing on the packet). **17** Drain, reserving the cooking water, and toss through the hare ragù, adding a touch of butter if you like, plus a little of the water to loosen. **18** Finish with the rest of the grated cacao.

Serves 6

hare 1, cut into 12 pieces

plain flour 50g

sea salt and freshly ground black pepper

olive oil 2 tablespoons

onion 1, chopped

carrot 1, chopped

celery 1 stalk, chopped

juniper berries 4, crushed to a paste

Chianti or other full-bodied red wine 1 bottle

good chicken stock 1 litre

bay leaf 1

fresh rosemary 1 sprig

90–100 per cent cacao 10g, grated

fresh or dried pappardelle 600–800g

butter a little

For the marinade:

full-bodied red wine 1 bottle

carrot 1, roughly chopped

onion 1, roughly chopped

celery 1 stalk, roughly chopped

black peppercorns 1 teaspoon, lightly crushed

juniper berries 1 teaspoon, lightly crushed

fresh rosemary 2 sprigs

bay leaf 1

garlic 1 clove

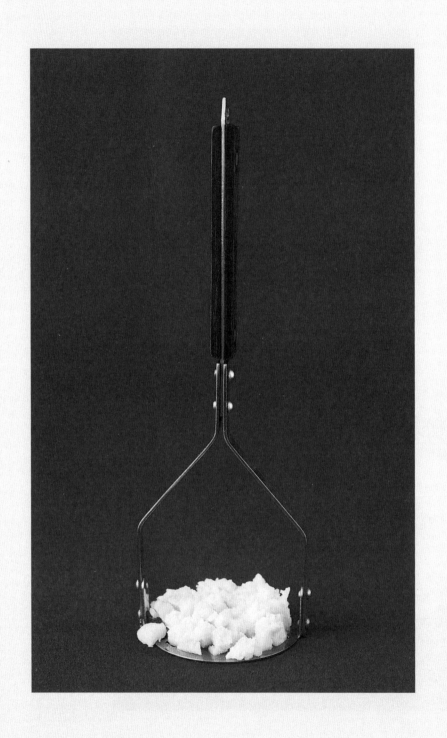

Gnocchi
x 4

Gnocchi – dumplings, mainly made with potato – should be very elegant and silky, like little clouds of flavour that dissolve in your mouth. If they become chewy it may be because you have added too much egg, or overworked the potato dough so it becomes too soft, and you have overcompensated by adding too much flour. Choose quite starchy potatoes such as Desiree, but make sure that you drain them well and then put them into a very low oven to steam until they are quite dry. If the potatoes are too wet they will keep on absorbing flour as you add it, and you only want to add as much flour as needed to bring the dough together.

The base recipe (makes 1kg of gnocchi)

Preheat the oven to 100°C/gas ½. Boil 1kg of whole Desiree potatoes in salted water until just tender, then, as soon as they are cool enough to handle, remove the skin and cut into quarters. Lay them on a baking tray, cover with foil (prick this with a fork, to make some small holes to allow air through) and put into the oven for 30 minutes, just long enough to dry the potato out. Have ready 320g of plain flour and 2 small lightly beaten eggs. Remove the potatoes from the oven and, while still hot, push them through a fine sieve into a bowl. Quickly, so that you don't allow the potatoes to cool, work in the eggs, a pinch of fine sea salt and about three-quarters of the flour to begin with, until you have a soft dough.

Very lightly dust your work surface and a tray with flour. Take pieces of the dough one at a time, roll them into long 'sausages' about 1cm in diameter, then cut each sausage into 1cm discs. Now, take each disc on to your forefinger and with the thumb of your other hand (once again lightly dusted with flour), lightly press and roll it in one movement so that it curls, then gently run the tines of a fork (again lightly floured) over the back of each piece. As you work, lay the gnocchi on the floured tray. Leave them to rest while you make your sauce.

The recipes overleaf make enough for 8, but any gnocchi you don't use you can put on a tray and freeze, then, when they are hard, you can pack them into bags, ready to defrost and drop into boiling water whenever you want to cook them.

With tomato, mozzarella and basil

This is *gnocchi alla Sorrentina*, so called because it is most famous in Sorrento, and it is my favourite.

1 Follow the recipe for potato gnocchi on page 175.
2 When you have good sweet cherry tomatoes, make the fresh tomato sauce on page 146. Otherwise, make the sauce with tinned tomatoes on page 147.
3 Roughly chop a buffalo mozzarella (about 125g).
4 Bring a big pan of salted water to the boil, put in the gnocchi and, as soon as they rise to the surface (after about a minute), lift them out with a slotted spoon, drain well and put them into the tomato sauce, adding around 10 leaves of fresh basil and 2 tablespoons of extra virgin olive oil. **5** Just before serving, add half the chopped mozzarella, stirring it in quickly. **6** Transfer to a warm serving dish and garnish with the rest of the mozzarella and some more basil leaves.

With Taleggio, radicchio tardivo and walnuts

1 Follow the recipe for potato gnocchi on page 175.
2 Preheat the oven to 180°C/gas 4. **3** Lay 3–4 tablespoons of walnuts on a baking tray and put into the oven for 7 minutes, moving the tray around occasionally so that the nuts turn golden all over.
4 Remove from the oven and allow to cool slightly, then rub the skins from the nuts and roughly chop them. **5** Slice the tops of the leaves from a head of radicchio – just take off about 5–6cm and keep these aside in a bowl. **6** Chop the rest of the leaves into pieces of about 1cm. **7** Heat about 100g of butter in a pan, add the chopped radicchio and sauté for a couple of minutes until soft, then season with sea salt and freshly ground black pepper. **8** Add half a glass (35ml) of white wine, bubble up to evaporate the alcohol, then add 300ml of double cream. **9** Bring to the boil, add 200g of Taleggio cheese and take off the heat, so that the cheese melts. **10** Bring a big pan of salted water to the boil, put in the gnocchi and, as soon as they rise to the surface (after about a minute), lift them out with a slotted spoon, drain well and put them into the sauce. **11** Spoon into a warm serving dish and garnish with the walnuts. **12** Season the reserved radicchio tips and toss with a little extra virgin oil, then arrange on the top.

With wild mushrooms

This is also beautiful with porcini, especially when they are well developed and spongy.

1 Follow the recipe for potato gnocchi on page 175. When in season, just use St George mushrooms; otherwise use whatever mixed wild mushrooms you like. **2** Melt around 50g of butter in a pan, add around 200g of cleaned and chopped mushrooms, season with sea salt and freshly ground black pepper and cook gently for a few minutes, then add half a glass (35ml) of white wine and bubble up to evaporate the alcohol. **3** Turn off the heat and add a small handful of chopped fresh parsley. **4** Have ready another 50g of diced butter. **5** Bring a big pan of salted water to the boil, put in the gnocchi and, as soon as they rise to the surface (after about a minute), lift them out with a slotted spoon, drain well and put them into the pan of mushrooms, with the diced butter, 30g of grated Parmesan and a small bunch of chopped fresh chives. **6** Toss around to coat, and serve.

With fish ragù

1 Follow the recipe for potato gnocchi on page 175. **2** Clean 500g of mussels and 500g of clams as on page 100. **3** Chop 3 squid pockets and 3 fillets of red mullet. **4** Heat some olive oil in a large pan, add 2 finely chopped cloves of garlic and a finely chopped mild red chilli, and cook gently and briefly. **5** Put in 6 peeled raw prawns, the squid, mussels and clams, add a glass (70ml) of white wine and cover with a lid. **6** Cook over a high heat until the mussels and clams open, then lift them out along with the prawns (but keep the juices in the pan). Discard any mussels or clams that stay closed and remove the rest from their shells. **7** Put another clove of garlic on a chopping board and crush into a paste with the back of a large knife. **8** Put a handful of fresh parsley leaves on top and chop finely, so that the garlic and parsley combine. **9** Add a ladleful of tomato passata to the shellfish juices, put in the red mullet and cook for around 5 minutes, then add the mussels and clams and season with sea salt and freshly ground black pepper if necessary. **10** Bring a big pan of salted water to the boil, put in the gnocchi and, as soon as they rise to the surface (after about a minute), lift them out with a slotted spoon, drain well and put them into the sauce, adding the parsley and garlic. **11** Garnish with the reserved prawns.

Sartu (baked rice with tomato, eggs, meatballs and cheese)

This is an elaborate, ceremonial rich man's Neapolitan rice cake filled with meatballs, eggs, tomato and cheese, which dates all the way back to the time when the Bourbon kings ruled Naples and Sicily. Yes, it takes a bit of work, but it is a great thing to make for a family party.

When I was filming in Naples, I made this for Marquis Carlo de Gregorio Cattaneo di Sant'Elia, whose family have been part of the Naples aristocracy for 200 years. It was such an exhilarating day. We arrived in Naples in the morning and I had to collect all the ingredients and assemble, bake and present it to the Marquis at 6p.m.

The food of the Bourbon era has always fascinated me because its great level of intricacy is so unlike anything before or afterwards in Italian cooking. It is said that Queen Maria Carolina, Marie Antoinette's sister, who became Queen of Naples and Sicily when she married the Bourbon King Ferdinand IV, didn't like the food at the royal court as it was too peasant-like, so she sent off to Paris for some chefs. When they arrived they were known as *les messieurs*, but after a few years, when the old chefs began to die and the Neapolitans who had worked under them took over, they could not be called 'monsieur' as they weren't French, so they became known as *monsu*. The Marquis had his own *monsu* as recently as the sixties, when sartu was served on special occasions, so when he gave me nine out of ten for my sartu, I took it as one of the great accolades of my cooking career. Only a genuine *monsu* would be allowed to score ten out of ten.

The name sartu comes from the French *'sur tout'*, meaning 'over everything', which refers to the rice casing, and it is a cousin of the much simpler Sicilian timballo. There are many versions, of course, but this one made with meatballs, boiled eggs and macaroni conjures up the richness of the Bourbon court.

You need a 25cm deep, round cake tin with a removable base.

1 Heat 1 tablespoon of olive oil in a large pan, add half the chopped onion and cook gently until soft and translucent. 2 Add the sausages and cook gently for 3 minutes to colour, then add the passata and simmer gently for 1 hour. If the liquid becomes too thick, add a little water. Take off the heat, remove the sausages and cut into 1cm slices. 3 Heat the rest of the olive oil in a large frying pan, add the rest of the chopped onion and the peas and cook for 3 minutes, until the peas are soft. 4 Transfer to a bowl and keep on one side. 5 Preheat the oven to 170°C/gas 3.

6 To make the meatballs, mix all the ingredients together, then form into balls (a little smaller than a golf ball). 7 Heat a little olive oil in a pan, put in the meatballs and brown all over. 8 Bring the stock to the boil in a large pan, add the rice and cook until just tender then drain and put into a bowl. Add a small ladleful of the reserved tomato sauce and stir in half the Parmesan. 9 Grease a 25cm deep round tin with the butter and tip in 2 tablespoons of the breadcrumbs, shaking the tin to cover all the surface. 10 Take three-quarters of the rice, spread some over the base (about 2.5cm thick), then use the rest to create a wall 2.5cm thick around the sides. Keep the rest of the rice on one side.

11 Scatter the sausage slices on top of the base layer of rice, together with the meatballs, sliced eggs, peas, mozzarella and the rest of the grated Parmesan and add another ladleful of sauce. 12 Cover with the rest of the rice in a flat layer. Sprinkle with the rest of the breadcrumbs. 13 Put into the preheated oven for 30 minutes, until golden on top. 14 Remove from the tin and turn out on to a large serving plate. 15 Spoon the rest of the tomato sauce over the top and scatter over the basil leaves.

Makes 1 x deep 25cm cake, enough for 10

olive oil 2 tablespoons
onion 1, finely chopped
good pork sausages 2
tomato passata 1 litre
fresh or frozen peas 200g
good chicken stock 1.5 litres
arborio rice 450g
Parmesan 200g, grated
butter 50g
dried breadcrumbs 3 tablespoons
eggs 2, hard-boiled and sliced
mozzarella 200g, sliced

For the meatballs:
minced meat (a mixture of pork, beef and veal, as you prefer) 300g
egg 1
crustless fresh bread 100g, broken into pieces
grated Parmesan 2 tablespoons
sea salt and freshly ground black pepper
olive oil a little, for frying
fresh basil leaves to garnish

Risotto
x 4

A risotto can be something that is completely sublime, but it is also the perfect fridge and store cupboard food that always allows you to feed your family something good and wholesome. Yes, ideally make your own stock, but if you don't have the time, you can buy good fresh stocks from the supermarket, and there are even very good cubes that you can keep in the cupboard. I am not ashamed to say I have fallen back on an emergency risotto many times, when as a family we have come home late from holiday, and I have pulled out a piece of cured sausage or chorizo and some cheese from the fridge, some peas or spinach from the freezer and a stock cube from the cupboard.

The base recipe (serves 6)

Bring 3 litres of good chicken stock to the boil, then turn down the heat so that it is barely simmering on the hob next to where you are making your risotto. Melt 80g of butter in a heavy-based pan, add a very finely chopped large onion and cook gently until soft and translucent, but not coloured. Turn up the heat a little, then put in 500g of superfino carnaroli rice and stir around with a wooden spoon until well coated in the butter and onion. The rice needs to be warm before you add 125ml of dry white wine. Bubble it up to evaporate the alcohol and continue to stir until the wine has virtually disappeared, then start adding your stock a ladleful at a time, just enough to cover the rice. Keep stirring the grains of rice around until they absorb the stock before adding the next ladleful. The rice will start to swell, and after about 15 minutes of stirring and adding stock, taste some of the grains – make sure you cool them a little first, as they will be very hot. The rice is ready when it has plumped up and is tender on the outside, but retains a slight firmness at the centre. Take the pan from the heat and allow it to rest and cool for a minute so that it will absorb the butter and cheese you are about to add without splitting. Quickly beat in 100g of cold, diced butter, then beat in 150g of grated Grana Padano or Parmesan and serve.

Each recipe overleaf also serves 6.

Saffron

This is unusual in that it is traditionally served with meat such as osso buco (page 252) or *scallopini milanese* (page 110).

Saffron is such a precious, expensive spice, requiring fields and fields of the saffron crocus to be harvested by hand and their stigmas dried to make the smallest amount of spice. Because it can command high prices, powdered saffron has always been open to adulteration with turmeric or paprika, while the threads from the saffron crocus have sometimes been substituted with threads of safflower (a different, thistle-like plant), beet or even silk. If the saffron is very cheap, be suspicious. Otherwise, genuine saffron threads should be unbroken and have a trumpet shape at one end, and when they are warmed, the aroma should be sweet and sublime and the colour they release into the rice will be golden and beautiful. I always think of this risotto as the personification of the colour yellow.

1 Follow the recipe on the previous page, but add a couple of pinches of saffron threads when you cook the onions.

Asparagus, wild garlic and Gorgonzola

This is a recipe to make in spring/early summer when asparagus and wild garlic are both in season.

1 Remove (but keep) the tips from a bunch of asparagus then chop the rest into 3mm pieces and keep these to one side. Blanch the tips in boiling salted water for 2 minutes, then drain and also keep aside. **2** Follow the recipe on the previous page, adding the chopped spears to the onion as it cooks, and use vegetable stock instead of chicken stock. **3** When the risotto is ready, beat in 50g of butter, 75g of Parmesan, 40g of Gorgonzola and about 10 finely chopped leaves of wild garlic. **4** Decorate with the asparagus tips and crumble another 40g of Gorgonzola on top.

Lemon, squid, chilli and fennel

1 You need 350g of squid pockets. **2** Chop 150g as finely as possible (ideally to a size similar to rice grains) and cut the rest into strips. **3** Put a clove of garlic on a chopping board and crush into a paste with the back of a large knife. **4** Put a handful of fresh parsley leaves on top and chop finely, so that the garlic and parsley combine. Keep to one side. **5** Heat some olive oil in a large pan, add a chopped onion, a finely chopped clove of garlic, half a hot red chilli and a finely chopped medium fennel bulb. **6** Add 450g of superfino carnaroli rice. **7** Follow the recipe on page 181, but use 2.5 litres of fish stock. **8** Five minutes before the rice is ready, add the juice of half a lemon and continue to cook until the rice is tender but al dente. **9** Meanwhile, heat a little olive oil in a sauté pan, add the rest of the chopped chilli and the strips of squid and sauté for 1 minute, then add half a glass (35ml) of white wine and bubble up to evaporate the alcohol. Keep to one side. **10** Finish with the parsley and garlic. **11** Take the pan of risotto off the heat, stir in the finely chopped squid and beat in 100g of butter. **12** Taste and season with sea salt, freshly ground black pepper and a little more lemon juice to taste. Serve garnished with the reserved sautéd squid.

Guinea fowl and black truffle

1 Preheat the oven to 180°C/gas 4. **2** Separate 2 guinea fowl into breasts, legs and wings. **3** Heat some olive oil in a large pan, add the guinea fowl pieces and sauté until the skin is golden and crispy. **4** Take out and reserve. **5** Add a chopped onion, a chopped carrot and a chopped stalk of celery to the pan with a sprig of fresh rosemary and a bay leaf and cook gently until the onion is soft and translucent, then add a glass (70ml) of white wine and bubble up to evaporate the alcohol. **6** Put the pieces of guinea fowl back into the pan and add around 500ml of good chicken stock (keep back a little in case you need it later). **7** Cover with a lid and put into the preheated oven for 45 minutes. **8** Remove from the oven and discard the herbs. **9** Lift out the guinea fowl and strip the meat from the bones. **10** Put the pan on the hob and reduce the liquid to a sauce consistency, then put back the guinea fowl meat. **11** Make the risotto as on page 181, but use 450g of rice. **12** After 10 minutes of adding the stock and stirring, put in the guinea fowl and its sauce, adding a little more stock if necessary. **13** Beat in 100g of butter and 150g of grated Parmesan. **14** Spoon into a warm serving dish and garnish, if you like, with a little grated black truffle.

The Saturday Pizza

To me, pizza is not an everyday food. It is something special. You go out to somewhere that makes only pizza in a wood-fired oven, and nothing else, or you make it at home. By turning it into something to pull out of the freezer any time, I don't believe we have done the pizza any favours. It should be a light, fresh, crispy flagship of the Mediterranean diet, not something that is so often heavy or flabby or laden with preservatives.

A good pizza begins with the dough. The key is to let it prove slowly overnight in the fridge and then allow it to rise a little more as it comes gently to room temperature over another four hours. If you make the dough at the last minute and put it somewhere warm to prove, it can puff up too quickly, then when it is baked it has no texture and becomes like a biscuit, whereas a dough that has proved slowly will give you a pizza that is crisp but light and characterful.

An Italian's natural instinct is to be purist about what to put on a pizza, so if someone suggests cauliflower or pulled pork as a topping, the first reaction is 'no way', but I have tasted both and they have been incredible. Who is to say who is right and who is wrong? It shows how far my ideas have turned around that sometimes I think being steeped in the knowledge and background of a food can actually limit you, whereas someone who is not bounded by the same cultural respect can come up with an idea that is exceptional. The world is constantly changing and food is evolving with it, so it seems foolish to me not to embrace that revolution. The only criteria can be whether you like something, or you don't.

The truth is pizza has never been defined as one thing: the earliest references are to a sort of flattened bread, focaccia or cake, which was born out of having a few basic ingredients to make a dough. It could be thick or thin, sweet or savoury, and may well have been covered in various toppings long before 1889, when it is said that the first tomato, mozzarella and basil pizza was made, to represent the colours of the Italian flag for a visit to Naples by King Umberto I and his queen, Margherita.

All of that said, my favourite pizza is still a good margherita. There was a camping site my brother and I used to go to sometimes with my grandad for a few days in the summer, where they would make pizza two or three times a week: pizza margherita and lemonade or beer, that was it, but it still seems to me that was some of the best pizza I ever had, especially as my grandad let us drink a beer with lemonade in it – 'But don't tell Nonna.'

And we have a photo of Margherita eating her first namesake pizza. A few years ago she had a new immunotherapy treatment for grasses, and the bonus was that she was no longer allergic to tomatoes, as long as they are cooked. What was amazing was that although the taste was something quite new to her, she remembered the smell as something very familiar, because the aroma of a great tomato is very powerful.

So the recipe I have given here is for a margherita, but you can build the toppings on the tomato sauce as you like. Saturday night is pizza night for the staff at Locanda, and we always make a variety of them.

Whatever you choose, the most important thing is not to add too many ingredients. Be sparing. If you crowd the top of the pizza you take away the heat, and it won't crisp up properly. And avoid ingredients that have too much moisture in them, as you don't want to turn the surface into a swimming pool in the oven. So if you buy your mozzarella in water, make sure you slice and drain it well. Cow's milk mozzarella is fine, as the best buffalo mozzarella is wasted unless you add it after the pizza comes out of the oven, in which case it is beautiful dotted over the top with some fresh basil. And if you are adding Parma ham, I also think this is better added after the pizza is baked.

Toppings

Before the pizzas go into the oven, you could add some blanched spinach and sautéd mushrooms, cooked ham, or some drained, tinned tuna and thinly sliced chilli and red onion. Alternatively, add some 'nduja (soft spicy salami), and when the pizzas come out of the oven dot some burrata over the top.

If you prefer no tomato sauce, you could add some blanched broccoli to the mozzarella, strip some fresh Italian sausages of their casings and sauté the meat in a pan to brown it, then scatter it over the top before the pizzas go into the oven. As another alternative to tomato sauce we sometimes make a soft pumpkin purée by roasting the pumpkin as on pages 84-5 and then blending it with a little water. Then we spread it over the dough, to mimic what the tomato sauce normally does. We add some pieces of Taleggio cheese and some potatoes that we have boiled, drained well so that they dry out, and then crumbled. When the pizza comes out of the oven, if everyone is really lucky, during the truffle season our supplier in Umbria, Carlo Caporicci, may have sent a little spare black truffle to grate over the top, and it is delicious.

The Saturday Pizza

1 Mix all the ingredients for the dough with 300ml of water (at room temperature). **2** Divide into four, then roll each piece into a ball and put on a tray, spacing them well apart. **3** Cover with clingfilm and put into the fridge overnight, where they will expand slightly. **4** Four hours before you want to bake the pizza, remove the balls of dough from the fridge and allow them to come slowly to room temperature. During this time they will prove a little more.

5 Preheat the oven to 220°C/gas 7 and put in a baking tray or trays to heat up – if you have some baking stones, better still. **6** Dust your work surface lightly with flour. **7** Take each ball of dough and gently push and stretch it with your fingertips until it is about 3–4mm thick. **8** Spoon a ladleful of tomato sauce on to each one and spread over the surface. **9** Dot some mozzarella over the top. **10** Drizzle each pizza with a tablespoon of extra virgin olive oil and finish with a pinch of dried oregano. **11** Slide the pizzas, two at a time, on to your hot trays or stones and bake for 10 minutes, until the edges turn dark brown and the mozzarella has melted. **12** Remove them from the oven and scatter over some basil leaves.

Makes 4 round pizzas

For the dough:

00 flour 500g, plus extra for dusting

fresh yeast 4g

extra virgin olive oil 1 tablespoon

fine sea salt 1 teaspoon

For the topping:

tomato sauce made with tinned tomatoes (see page 147) 4 ladlefuls

cow's milk mozzarella 4 x 125g

extra virgin olive oil 4 tablespoons

dried oregano a little

fresh basil leaves a handful

Ricotta dumplings (gnudi)
x 4

Fresh ricotta is such an undervalued ingredient that I feel has yet to reach its full potential in terms of popularity. It is beautiful by itself but it is also a good carrier of other flavours, so it really comes into its own in the form of these delicate dumplings.

The point about ricotta, is yes, it is an Italian idea, but since it is simply made by 're-cooking' whey, skimming off the proteins which rise to the top and then draining them, it can be made wherever there is sheep or cow's milk of exceptional quality – I have even had fresh ricotta made with camel's milk in Dubai, which was really quite heavy and rich but incredible. So it seems ridiculous to me to have a ricotta travel from Liguria when there are British dairies making quite special ricotta from grass-fed cows as a by-product of their cheeses.

The base recipe (makes 18 gnudi: enough for 6 people)

First, the ricotta needs to be drained of all its moisture so that it is completely dry before you make the dumplings. So, put 600g of ricotta into a colander over a bowl, put a plate on top and weight it down with a tin of beans for a few hours to dry it out. Mix with 60g of grated Parmesan and 3 egg yolks. In a separate clean bowl, whisk 6 egg whites until they form stiff peaks. Fold into the ricotta mixture, as if you were making a soufflé (at this point you can also fold in any of the flavourings overleaf). Scoop into 18 oval-shaped dumplings or quenelles. Have ready a shallow bowl of semolina, dust the dumplings in it, then lay them on a tray and put them back into the fridge to rest and firm up for at least 4 hours or overnight. When ready to cook, bring a pan of salted water to the boil, then turn down the heat so that it is just under the boil. Lower in the gnudi for about 3 minutes, until they float to the top. Lift out with a slotted spoon and serve. You can also cook them this way in advance, and then reheat them very briefly in the oven, just for about 10 minutes at 170°C/gas 3 before serving.

If you want the gnudi to be gluten-free, don't dust them with semolina, and only rest them in the fridge for an hour, then lay them in batches on a sheet of baking paper (space them well apart), put them into a steamer and steam for 10 minutes. Lift out and cover with clingfilm while you steam the rest.

With peas

You can make this with a mix of baby broad beans and peas, if you prefer, or even just broad beans.

1 Make the gnudi mixture as on the previous page up to the point of shaping into dumplings. **2** Cook 250g of fresh or frozen peas and drain them. **3** Tip half of them on to some kitchen paper and pat them dry, as you want to remove all the excess moisture, then fold into the gnudi mixture. **4** When ready to serve, heat 2 tablespoons of olive oil in a pan, add a finely chopped spring onion and the rest of the drained peas, plus 4 tablespoons of water, cook for 10 minutes, then either transfer to a blender or use a hand blender to whiz into a bright green purée, adding 2 more tablespoons of extra virgin olive oil as you go. **5** Cook the gnudi as on the previous page, then serve on top of the pea purée and garnish with a few pea shoots.

Spinach

1 Make the gnudi mixture as on the previous page up to the point of shaping into dumplings. **2** Blanch 120g of spinach in boiling salted water for a couple of minutes. **3** Drain it under cold running water, then squeeze it to remove as much moisture as possible. **4** Chop and drain further on kitchen paper to remove all the remaining moisture, then fold into the gnudi mixture. **5** When ready to serve, warm up some tomato passata (see page 146 for homemade) in a pan. **6** Cook the gnudi as on the previous page and serve on top of the tomato passata.

Mushroom

1 Make the gnudi mixture as on page 191, up to the point of shaping into dumplings. **2** Heat some olive oil in a sauté pan, add a finely chopped clove of garlic and sauté briefly, taking care not to burn it. **3** Add 150g of mixed wild mushrooms, season with sea salt and freshly ground black pepper, and cook gently until most of the moisture has evaporated from the mushrooms. **4** Finely chop and further drain on kitchen paper to remove all the excess moisture, then fold into the gnudi mixture. **5** When ready to serve, melt a knob of butter in a pan, add a whole clove of garlic and sauté until golden, lift out and put in another 100g of mixed wild mushrooms, sauté briefly, then add half a glass (35ml) of white wine and bubble up to evaporate. If you have some radicchio tardivo (when in season), just cut off the tips and season with sea salt and freshly ground black pepper, then add to the pan. **6** Cook the gnudi as on page 191 and serve with the wild mushrooms and radicchio, if using.

Black truffle

Try to buy a good truffle paste, which should have little else in it but pieces of truffle and olive oil.

1 Make the gnudi mixture as on page 191, up to the point of shaping into dumplings. **2** Put 100g of black truffle paste in a colander and drain off the excess oil then fold into the gnudi mixture. **3** Cook the gnudi as on page 191 and serve with grated Parmesan and a little grated black truffle.

If you like, you could serve these with a sauce made with Taleggio cheese: melt 60g of butter in a pan, add 60g of plain flour and cook gently for 3 minutes to make a roux, then whisk in a litre of milk a little at a time. Bring to the boil, season with sea salt and freshly ground black pepper, then turn down to a simmer until you have a thick sauce. Take off the heat, add 200g of Taleggio cheese (cut into pieces) and keep stirring until the cheese has melted into the sauce.

When I go to buy
fish it is never with a
recipe. You have to
look at what is on the
stall or the counter
and see which
seafood is talking
to you. Then decide
how to cook it. You
don't choose the fish.
It chooses you.

Favourite fish and seafood

Monkfish stew with tomatoes, garlic, chilli and black olives

We call this *in potacchio*, which is a style of braising in wine, tomato, garlic, chilli and rosemary that is typical of the Marche region, not only for fish, but also chicken and rabbit. I find that people are really confident using monkfish to put into a stew like this, because apart from the central bone it has no other small bones to worry about.

1 Heat a little olive oil in a large pan. **2** Add the garlic, chilli, the sprigs of rosemary and the chopped rosemary, and sauté for 1 minute, taking care not to burn the garlic. **3** Add the olives and then the fish, and season. **4** Sauté everything together for 5 minutes, stirring, so that the chilli and garlic coats the fish. **5** Add the wine, bubble up to evaporate the alcohol, then add the fish stock, tomato passata and tomatoes. **6** Cover with a lid and cook for another 10 minutes, until the fish is tender, then discard the sprigs of rosemary and spoon into a warmed serving dish. **7** Cut the toasted bread roughly into squares and serve the stew on top. **8** Drizzle with the extra virgin olive oil.

Serves 6

olive oil

garlic 3 cloves, finely chopped

whole mild red chilli 1, finely chopped

fresh rosemary 3 sprigs

finely chopped rosemary leaves 1 tablespoon

black olives 4 tablespoons, stones removed

monkfish fillet 1.5kg, cut into chunks

sea salt and freshly ground black pepper

white wine 1 glass (70ml)

good fish stock 500ml

tomato passata 4 tablespoons

cherry tomatoes 15, halved

To serve:

good bread 6 large slices, toasted

extra virgin olive oil 3 tablespoons

Roast John Dory with asparagus, potatoes, shallots and butter

This is quite an elegant dish to make when English asparagus is in season. John Dory was one of the first sea fish that I got to know as a young chef. Our family hotel and restaurant was right on the shore of Lake Comabbio, which was fed by the rivers running down from the mountains, so apart from salt cod, sardines, mackerel and the red prawns which came in each week from San Remo, the only fish I ever saw in the kitchen there, or at home, were freshwater varieties: eel, carp, perch and pike, which have a very different flavour and texture to sea fish.

It was only when I started my first real job at Il Passatore restaurant in Varese that I got to appreciate the delicate beauty of fish such as John Dory, sea bream and sea bass. Whereas meat cooking can be a muscular, virile thing, preparing and cooking fish in a way that preserves its essential nature requires a more delicate touch.

Later, during my time cooking in Paris, fish was often served with beurre blanc (the classic reduction of cream, butter, white wine, vinegar and shallot), which was another new idea for an Italian more used to serving it simply grilled, with nothing to distract from its essential flavour, except for a piece of lemon. I think that must have been in the back of my mind the first time I made this, but I also wanted to add some potato, as well as asparagus, which is in season at the same time as John Dory, and finish with the flavours that are so much a part of my identity: parsley and garlic.

(see picture on next page)

1 Put the potatoes into salted water, bring to the boil, then turn down to a simmer until just tender, but still quite firm. **2** Drain them, allow to cool, then peel and chop them. **3** Stand the asparagus upright in a pan of boiling salted water – make sure the more delicate tips are clear of the water, so that they steam, rather than boil and become too soft. **4** Cook for about 5–6 minutes, until the spears are just tender, drain and arrange horizontally in a warmed serving dish.

5 Meanwhile, to make the sauce, heat a couple of pieces of the butter in a pan, add the shallots and cook gently until soft and translucent. **6** Add the white wine and bubble up to evaporate the alcohol. **7** Add the vinegar and reduce by half, then add the cream and continue cooking until the sauce has reduced by half again, and is creamy but not too thick. **8** Whisk in the rest of the butter until it has been completely absorbed and the sauce is rich and buttery, then stir in the chopped potatoes, season as necessary and take off the heat.

9 Put the clove of garlic on a chopping board and crush it into a paste with the back of a large knife. **10** Put the parsley on top and chop finely, so that the garlic and parsley combine and release their flavours into each other. Keep to one side.

11 Heat some olive oil in a large sauté pan, put in the John Dory fillets, season with salt and when the underside turns golden, turn them over, season again with salt and cook for 1 minute. **12** Sprinkle in the lemon juice, then lift out the fillets with a fish slice and place on top of the asparagus spears. **13** Add the parsley and garlic to the sauce and spoon over the asparagus. **14** Finish with the hard-boiled eggs.

Serves 6

potatoes 2 large, skin on

asparagus about 24 thick spears

sea salt and freshly ground black pepper

butter 250g, diced

shallots 3, finely chopped

white wine ½ glass (35ml)

white wine vinegar 1 tablespoon

double cream 35ml

garlic 1 clove

fresh flat-leaf parsley a small bunch

olive oil

John Dory 3 (around 1kg each), filleted

lemon juice of 1

hard-boiled eggs 2, separated into whites and yolks, then chopped and pushed through a fine sieve

Baked whole fish

The dream of my life is still to live near the sea and go out each day with my boat and a rod and catch just enough fish for supper. But when Plaxy and I are on holiday in Puglia the next best thing is to go out each day and see what fresh fish there is: maybe a dorade, a gilt-head bream, a John Dory, or some little sea bass (warm-water Mediterranean fish are always smaller than ones from cold water). Then my favourite thing is to bake the fish whole on the bone, maybe with some tomato and olive oil, rosemary, fennel, garlic, chilli, even some sliced potatoes.

Cooking fish on the bone conserves the natural flavour in a more profound way, since it cooks from the outside in. The skin protects the most sensitive flesh around the bone, which because it has no direct contact with the heat or with oil doesn't pick up flavours in the same way as it would do if you pan-fried it.

1 Preheat the oven to 180°C/gas 4. **2** Mix all the vegetables with the garlic, chilli and parsley in a large roasting tray. **3** Season and drizzle with half the olive oil. **4** Season the cavity of the sea bass. Slice one of the lemons and put inside, along with the rosemary. **5** Lay the fish on top of the vegetables and pour the white wine over the top. Sprinkle on some sea salt and bake in the preheated oven for about 45 minutes, depending on the size of the fish. To test that it is cooked, insert the tip of a knife under the fillets and it should come out hot. **6** To serve, remove the skin and then lift off the top piece of fillet to one side. Then carefully lift off the piece of belly fillet – this is where most of the bones are concentrated, so lift these out. Now you can run a fork under the backbone to release it and lift it out, then remove the remaining pieces of fillet. **7** Drizzle the fish with the juice of the remaining lemon and the rest of the extra virgin olive oil and serve with the vegetables.

Serves 6

small courgettes 2 , sliced

medium potatoes 3, sliced

onion 1, sliced

fennel bulbs 2, sliced

garlic 5 cloves, whole

green chilli 1, chopped

sprigs parsley 2

sea salt and freshly ground black pepper

olive oil 6 tablespoons

large sea bass 1, around 1.5kg, cleaned

lemons 2

rosemary 2 sprigs

white wine 1 glass (70ml)

Fillet of cod with chickpeas, mussels and 'nduja

'Nduja from Calabria – soft, spicy, spreading salami made with local red chillies – is one of the latest Italian ingredients to jump almost overnight from something that was little known outside the region of production to a fashionable ingredient on every menu. I have always found it a fascinating flavour and texture, which works brilliantly with chickpeas and seafood. If you are using jarred or tinned chickpeas, try to buy organic ones, or read the labels to check there are no unwanted ingredients such as thickeners.

1 Soak 300g of dried chickpeas in water overnight, then drain. **2** Heat some olive oil in a pan, add the finely chopped onion, carrot and celery, then add the chickpeas and cover with water. **3** Bring to the boil, then turn down to a simmer until tender and drain. **4** Preheat the oven to 180°C/gas 4. **5** Finely chop one of the cloves of garlic. **6** Heat a little olive oil in a large pan, put in the garlic and sauté it briefly, making sure you don't let it burn. **7** Add the mussels and the white wine. **8** Cover with a lid and cook over a high heat, shaking the pan a couple of times, until the mussels open. **9** Discard any that don't open. **10** Lift the mussels from the cooking liquid and keep to one side, then add the tomato passata to the pan. **11** Break up the 'nduja with your fingers and add to the pan with the chickpeas, then continue to cook until you have a sauce consistency. If you feel it isn't thickening enough, crush a few of the chickpeas and this will help.

12 Take half the mussels from their shells (keep the rest for garnish) and return to the pan, then transfer all the contents to an ovenproof dish. **13** Heat a little more olive oil in a large sauté pan. **14** Season the cod and pan-fry on the skin side only until golden. **15** Lift out and place on top of the mussel and 'nduja sauce skin side up. **16** Garnish with the reserved mussels in their shells, and put into the preheated oven for about 5 minutes, until the cod has cooked through.
17 Meanwhile, put the remaining clove of garlic on a chopping board and crush it into a paste with the back of a large knife. **18** Put the parsley leaves on top and chop finely, so that the garlic and parsley combine and release their flavours into each other. **19** Remove the dish from the oven, sprinkle with the parsley and garlic and a little extra virgin olive oil and serve.

Serves 6

dried chickpeas 500g (see page 44), or good jarred or tinned ones, rinsed and drained

olive oil

onion 1, finely chopped

carrot 1, finely chopped

celery 1 stalk, finely chopped

garlic 2 cloves

mussels 1kg, cleaned (see page 100)

white wine 1 glass (70ml)

tomato passata 4 tablespoons

'nduja 200g

cod fillet 6 pieces (around 200g each)

fresh parsley a small handful

extra virgin olive oil a little, to finish

Deep-fried monkfish with prawn mayonnaise

One time when Plaxy went to buy some monkfish
for dinner the ones she brought back were so tiny,
what was I going to do with them? I decided to make
something else for the main dish, and instead use the
monkfish to make these little goujons as a starter.
You could put them out with plain mayonnaise
or aïoli, but they are really delicious with prawn
mayonnaise, which you can also use in other ways.
We spooned it on to fresh tuna burgers for the boys
in the kitchen one evening and it went down very well.

1 Heat a little olive oil in a pan, add the prawns in their shells and sauté for a couple of minutes, until the shells turn red. **2** Add the tomato purée and sauté for a couple more minutes. **3** Add enough water just to cover the prawns and simmer for 10 minutes. **4** Take off the heat, then push through a fine sieve into a clean pan and allow to bubble up and reduce until you have a rich, thick purée. **5** Take off the heat and keep to one side.

6 To make the mayonnaise, in a bowl whisk the egg yolk with the vinegar and mustard and then slowly, slowly begin to add the vegetable oil, whisking continuously and only adding more when the last addition has been incorporated. If it feels too thick, whisk in a little cold water (this will also help to stop it splitting). **7** Stir in 2 tablespoons of the reserved prawn purée to begin with, taste and season, and add more of the prawn purée if you need more flavour. **8** Finally, add lemon juice to taste and a touch of cayenne pepper, and keep the mayonnaise in the fridge until ready to serve.

9 Have the semolina in a shallow bowl, season it and pass each strip of monkfish through it, shaking off the excess. **10** Heat some vegetable oil to 180°C in a deep-fryer (alternatively, heat the oil in a large pan, no more than a third full – if you don't have a kitchen thermometer, drop a little flour into the oil and it will sizzle very gently). **11** Lower in the coated monkfish and deep-fry until golden. **12** Lift out and drain on kitchen paper. **13** Sprinkle with sea salt and serve with the prawn mayonnaise.

Serves 6

olive oil

raw prawns 200g, in their shells

tomato purée 1 teaspoon

semolina 200g

monkfish fillets 600g, cut into strips

vegetable or seed oil for deep-frying

For the prawn mayonnaise:

egg yolk 1

white wine vinegar 1 tablespoon

English mustard 1 teaspoon

vegetable oil 500ml

sea salt and freshly ground black pepper

lemon juice about 1 tablespoon, or to taste

cayenne pepper a pinch

Sea bream baked in salt

Baking fish in a salt crust is one of the oldest of cooking methods, which at one time meant digging a pit in the ground, putting in the fish in its coat of salt, piling the earth over it and then lighting a fire on top. In the heat the salt hardened, keeping the fish inside nice and juicy as it cooked. The same thing happens inside your oven, and the beauty of it is that the salt seasons the fish only very lightly, so there is nothing overly salty about it when you crack the salt crust and lift it out, and because the fish is cooked whole it has that extra succulence and depth of flavour that cooking on the bone gives.

I think fish baked like this is fantastic served with whatever iron-y greens are in season: spinach, broccoli or Swiss chard, blanched briefly, drained and then sautéd in olive oil, with some chopped spring onions, garlic and a little chilli, if you like.

1 Preheat the oven to 180°C/gas 4. **2** Put all the herbs and the garlic into a blender and whiz briefly until finely chopped. **3** Mix with the salt. **4** Spread a quarter of the salt mixture over the base of a roasting tin. **5** Put in the fish and cover completely with the rest of the salt mixture. **6** Put into the preheated oven and bake for 30–40 minutes. **7** To check the fish is cooked, break off a little of the salt, which will have formed a crust, and insert the tip of a sharp knife into the fish. It should come out hot. If not, continue to bake it for a bit longer. **8** Remove the roasting tin from the oven and, with a spoon, crack the salt crust all the way around the edge – you should be able to lift it off in one piece. **9** Take the skin from the fish, then lift off the pieces of fillet and remove the bones as on page 205. **10** Serve drizzled with a little olive oil and lemon juice.

Serves 6

fresh parsley leaves 3 bunches

fresh basil leaves 3 bunches

fresh sage leaves 1 bunch

fresh rosemary leaves 1 bunch

garlic 1 clove

sea salt 4kg

sea bream 2 (1kg each), or 1 sea bass (2kg), cleaned, but with heads left on

To serve:

extra virgin olive oil

lemon juice

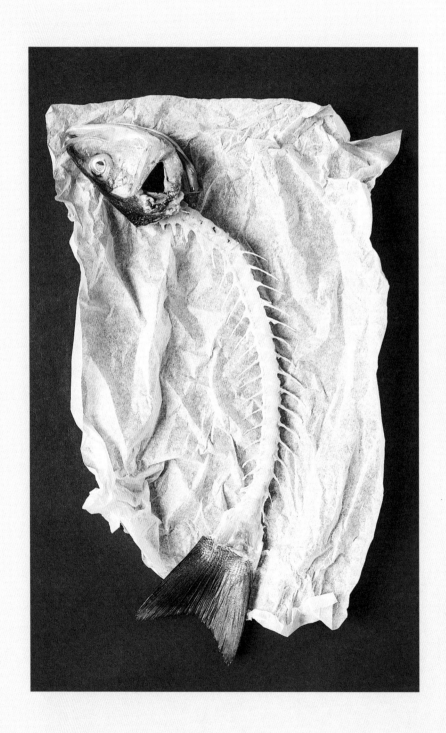

Fish soup/stew
x 4

All around the Mediterranean coast you find fish soups, or
stews, whichever you prefer to call them, made with whatever
seafood is caught locally. I wish I could encourage everybody
to try these dishes because they are brilliant to share – so
I have turned two of these recipes into celebrations of the
fantastic seafood fished around the coasts of Scotland and
of Cornwall. I have also given a recipe for a generic Italian one
(though in reality there is no such thing, as every region has
its own speciality), as well as a Ligurian *buridda* which has no
shellfish. Instead, the injection of flavour comes from dried
mushrooms and walnuts, ingredients which are justified by
the closeness of the mountains to the sea.

The Cornish recipe includes razor clams, which I love: such
beautiful things, so weird and prehistoric. To prepare them,
run a sharp knife down the length of each shell so that you can
open it out like a book, then remove the black vein from the
clam, again with the tip of a sharp knife, but leave each one in
its shell, then rinse well under cold running water.

The base recipe:
For all the soups apart from the *buridda* the stock is made in
the same way; the only variation is the choice of fish. Take the
fillets from 2 large red gurnard, keep these for the soup, and
reserve the heads and bones. Heat some olive oil in a large
pan, add a sliced onion, a chopped stalk of celery, a chopped
carrot, a sprig of fresh parsley and a bay leaf and cook gently
until the onion is soft and translucent. Don't add salt, as you
can season the stew/soup later. Add the fish bones and cook
for another few minutes, then put in a tablespoon of tomato
purée and keep stirring for another 3–4 minutes. Pour in
2.5 litres of water, bring to the boil, then turn down to a
simmer for 15 minutes. Pass the stock through a fine sieve and
keep to one side.

Each soup/stew overleaf makes enough for 6. Serve in
bowls with good bread, or bruschetta brushed with olive oil
and garlic.

Scottish

First make the base on page 213. Then I suggest a filleted brill, each fillet cut into 6 pieces, 3 medium lobsters, 6 medium langoustines, 1kg of clams and 1kg of mussels (prepared as on page 100) and 6 large scallops (out of their shells).

1 Heat some olive oil in a pan, add 2 finely chopped cloves of garlic and 2 finely chopped hot red chillies and cook for a few minutes, taking care not to burn the garlic. **2** Put in the brill and reserved gurnard fillets, add a glass (70ml) of white wine and bubble up to evaporate the alcohol, cook for a few minutes, then add 5 chopped tomatoes, cook for a few more minutes and add the base. **3** Bring to the boil, then turn down to a simmer and add the rest of the fish and shellfish. **4** Cook for 5 minutes, discard any mussels and clams that don't open, taste and season with sea salt and freshly ground black pepper. **5** Transfer to a warmed serving bowl (or, if the soup seems a bit too thin, lift the seafood into the bowl, then bubble up the liquid in the pan to reduce it a little before pouring it over the top. **6** To finish, crush a clove of garlic and chop it into a paste together with a handful of parsley leaves, scatter the mixture over the stew/soup, and, if you like, add a little drizzle of extra virgin olive oil.

Cornish

First make the base on page 213, but use 2 red mullet instead of the red gurnard. Then I would use a large, cleaned cuttlefish, sliced, and a small turbot, filleted, 1kg of monkfish fillets, 12 razor clams prepared as on the previous page and 500g of cleaned squid.

1 Heat some olive oil in a pan, add 2 finely chopped cloves of garlic and 2 finely chopped hot red chillies (be a bit careful, as you don't want to overpower the fish). **2** Cook for a few minutes, taking care not to burn the garlic. **3** Put in the cuttlefish, put the lid on the pan and cook gently for 10 minutes, to release the water from the cuttlefish. **4** Add the turbot and monkfish and a glass (70ml) of white wine and bubble up to evaporate the alcohol. **5** Turn down the heat and cook for another 10 minutes, then add 5 chopped tomatoes, cook for a few minutes, add the base, bring to the boil, then turn down to a simmer for 10 minutes. **6** Put in the razor clams, reserved mullet fillets and squid. Cook for 5 more minutes, or until the squid is tender. **7** Taste and season with sea salt and freshly ground black pepper, then transfer to a large, warmed serving bowl. **8** Crush a clove of garlic and chop it into a paste together with a handful of parsley leaves, then scatter over the stew/soup and drizzle with some extra virgin olive oil.

Italian

Make the base on page 213 but substitute scorpion fish if you are in Italy. I suggest 500g of baby octopus, cleaned, 12 red prawns (head and tails left on, but the rest of the shells removed), 1kg of clams and 1kg of mussels (cleaned as on page 100), 2 red mullet and 500g of baby cod or cod (in Italy the fish is always smaller).

1 Heat some olive oil in a pan, add 2 finely chopped cloves of garlic and 2 finely chopped hot red chillies and cook for a few minutes, taking care not to burn the garlic. **2** Put in the octopus, add a glass (70ml) of white wine and bubble up to evaporate the alcohol, then add 5 chopped tomatoes and cook for a few more minutes. **3** Add enough of the base to just cover the octopus and let it stew for 15 minutes, then add the rest of the fish (including the reserved gurnard fillets) and shellfish and simmer for another 10 minutes. **4** Taste and season with sea salt and freshly ground black pepper. **5** Lift out the fish and shellfish to a warmed serving bowl, then bubble up the liquid in the pan to reduce it a little and pour over the top. **6** Crush a clove of garlic and chop it into a paste with a handful of fresh parsley leaves, then scatter the mixture over the stew/soup. If you like, add a little drizzle of extra virgin olive oil.

Ligurian buridda

You need around 4 salted anchovies, 500g of cleaned and sliced cuttlefish, 500g of monkfish, 500g of octopus, cleaned and chopped, 500g of red gurnard and 500g of turbot fillets. Soak 2 heaped tablespoons of dried porcini in water for an hour, then drain and chop. Wash, dry and fillet the salted anchovies.

1 Heat some olive oil in a large pan, add 2 finely chopped onions, a chopped carrot, a chopped stalk of celery, a finely chopped clove of garlic and a handful of finely chopped parsley leaves. **2** Cook gently for a couple of minutes, until the onion is soft and translucent. **3** Add the anchovy fillets and stir until they 'melt'. **4** Using a pestle and mortar, crush the mushrooms, add 2 heaped tablespoons of toasted walnuts and work into a paste. **5** Add this to the vegetables and sauté for about 3 minutes. **6** Add all the fish, with a glass (70ml) of white wine, and bubble up to evaporate the alcohol, then put in 5 chopped tomatoes and cover with a lid. **7** Leave to braise for 30 minutes, then lift out any fish that is cooked to a warm plate or bowl. **8** Put this back when the octopus and cuttlefish are tender, for just long enough to heat through. **9** Transfer to a warmed serving bowl. **10** Crush a clove of garlic and chop with a handful of fresh parsley leaves, then scatter over the stew and drizzle with extra virgin olive oil.

Stewed cuttlefish with peas and mint

Cuttlefish stewed like this has a very special texture, tenderness and umami taste. It is typical of Venice, where it is served with soft white polenta, cooked in water and salt for around 45 minutes. White polenta is traditional with fish, and golden polenta with meat – but it is also good with polenta that has been allowed to become cold and then fried (see page 263) or with some toasted bread seasoned with olive oil and freshly ground black pepper.

1 Cut the cuttlefish into strips about 1cm wide. **2** Chop the tentacles. **3** Heat some olive oil in a large pan, add the onion and cook gently until soft and translucent. **4** Put in the cuttlefish and cook gently for 10 minutes, then add the bay leaves and the white wine and bubble up to evaporate the alcohol. **5** Add the tomato purée and just enough water to cover the cuttlefish. **6** Cover the pan with a lid and cook for 1 hour, then put in the peas and continue to cook for another 10 minutes. **7** Add the chopped mint, taste and season.

Serves 6

cuttlefish 2 large (about 1kg each), cleaned

olive oil

onion 1 large, finely chopped

bay leaves 2

white wine 1 glass (70ml)

tomato purée 3 tablespoons

fresh podded peas 300g

fresh mint leaves 1 small bunch, chopped

sea salt and freshly ground black pepper

Stewed octopus with artichoke and potatoes

I love this. I find kids, in particular, really like octopus if you introduce them early on to its very special texture and flavour. Jack loved the knobbly look of it, the taste, everything about it the first time he tried it when we were on holiday in Sardinia. When the artichoke, potato and octopus are all perfectly cooked, this is a beautiful little stew. The trick is to reserve the cooking water from the octopus, as this will be enriched with gelatine and when you add it back at the end it helps to give the sauce its unctuous consistency.

1 Bring a large pot of lightly salted water to the boil. **2** Add the bay leaves and one of the halves of onion, together with one half of the lemon and the celery. **3** Put in the octopus, bring to the boil, then turn down to a simmer for 40 minutes–1 hour. **4** Remove the octopus from the cooking water (but reserve this). **5** Chop the tentacles into two pieces and the head crossways into four, throwing away the eye section.

6 Finely chop one of the cloves of garlic and chop the remaining onion half. **7** Heat a little olive oil in a pan, add the onion, garlic and chilli and cook gently for about 2 minutes. **8** Add the prepared pieces of artichoke, season with sea salt and freshly ground black pepper, then add the white wine together with 2 ladlefuls of the reserved cooking water from the octopus. **9** Put in the pieces of octopus, the potatoes and tomato purée and cook gently for about 20 minutes, until the potatoes are tender.

10 Just before serving, put the remaining clove of garlic on a chopping board and crush it into a paste with the back of a large knife. **11** Put the parsley on top and chop finely, so that the garlic and parsley combine and release their flavours into each other. **12** Transfer the stew to a warmed serving dish, squeeze the remaining half of lemon over the top, scatter in the parsley and garlic mixture and drizzle with the extra virgin olive oil.

Serves 6

bay leaves	2
onion	1, halved
lemon	1, halved
celery	1 stalk, cut in half
octopus	1 (about 2kg), cleaned
garlic	2 cloves
olive oil	
green chilli	1, finely chopped
globe artichokes	6 small, prepared and halved as on page 63
sea salt and freshly ground black pepper	
white wine	½ a glass (35ml)
new potatoes	10, peeled and halved
tomato purée	1 tablespoon
fresh flat-leaf parsley	a small bunch
extra virgin olive oil	1 tablespoon

If we all ate 50 per cent less meat it would be a really good start. Eat less, but when we do eat meat, pay more attention to its quality and the welfare of the animal that has given it to us.

Grilled meats, roasts and stews

Griddled chicken thighs

These were always Margherita's favourite, which Plaxy would make for her, minus the chilli in the chimichurri-style sauce. They are great for the barbecue, put out with salads or roasted vegetables. Chicken thighs have so much more flavour than the breasts. Just trim off any overhanging pieces of skin and flatten the flesh so that it is a uniform thickness before you grill or barbecue them hard, skin side down. If you have any left over, they are brilliant cold in a sandwich with a little salad the next day.

1 Put the thighs on a chopping board. **2** Lay a sheet of clingfilm over the top and, with a rolling pin or a steak hammer, flatten the meat out a little. **3** Mix the garlic, rosemary, olive oil and chillies in a large bowl, put in the chicken and leave to marinate in the fridge for 12 hours or preferably overnight. **4** To make the sauce, mix all the ingredients in a bowl with 125ml water and leave to infuse in the fridge alongside the chicken. **5** When ready to cook, lift the chicken from the marinade, season it, then grill or barbecue, skin side down, until the skin is golden and the chicken is cooked through (roughly 10 minutes). **6** Lay in a serving dish and spoon the sauce over the top.

Serves 6

boneless chicken thighs 12 large, free-range or organic, skin on, trimmed (see intro)

garlic 3 cloves, sliced

fresh rosemary 3 sprigs

olive oil 3 tablespoons

hot red chillies 2, chopped

For the chimichurri-style sauce:

salt a good pinch

fresh parsley a small bunch, chopped

fresh oregano a small bunch, chopped

garlic 1 clove, finely chopped

mild red chillies 2, chopped

red wine vinegar 2 tablespoons

extra virgin olive oil 4 tablespoons

Giorgio's roast chicken

At home we like to roast chicken very simply. The
chicken is always organic because it is the only way
to be sure that the birds have had a decent life.
Otherwise, in intensive farming systems, you can't
verify how they are treated: chickens don't write
anonymous letters! When you have the time, the
supreme way of roasting a good chicken is to brine
it first, which makes a dramatic difference, keeping
the meat really moist and juicy. I like to roast some
potatoes and vegetables around the chicken as it
cooks. For six people I would mix a couple of onions
(quartered), 3 courgettes, 3 carrots and 3 stalks of
celery (all cut into chunks) in a bowl with 4 potatoes
(quartered), around 4 sprigs of rosemary and 10 cloves
of garlic. I would toss them all with 3 tablespoons of
olive oil, season them and then put them into the
roasting pan around the chicken. Halfway through
cooking I add a wine glass (70ml) of water.

1 Put all the brine ingredients into a pan with 3 litres of water and bring to the boil until the salt has dissolved, then take off the heat and leave to infuse as the brine cools down. **2** Put the chicken into a container just big enough to hold it, pour the brine over and leave in the fridge for at least 6 hours to tenderise and flavour the flesh. **3** Preheat the oven to 180°C/gas 4. **4** Remove the chicken from the brine, put into a roasting pan and roast for about 45 minutes, or until the juices run clear when you pierce the thighs with the tip of a sharp knife.

Serves 6

chicken 1 large (about 2kg), free-range or preferably organic

For the brine:

sea salt 120g

fresh rosemary 5 sprigs

bay leaves 4

black peppercorns 1 tablespoon

juniper berries 1 teaspoon

garlic 4 cloves

lemon peel of 1

Boned, stuffed chicken

This is a quite a ceremonial recipe, a version of which every northern Italian knows, and which is almost a part of my DNA. My grandmother was very good at roasts, and this would always be made with a capon: a male cockerel that had been neutered and fattened up. For a family feast we would usually have a little antipasti, then a risotto or pasta, and then afterwards everyone would have a slice or two of the roasted bird, wrapped in pancetta and stuffed with pork, apricots, mushrooms, chicken livers and chestnuts, collected from the woods above our house and roasted first. The last time I cooked a capon this way was at home in Italy with all the family for Christmas when my father and brother were still alive, though my brother was already ill, and they both loved it. So it has an even more special place in my memory bank.

In the UK it is not permitted to neuter male birds, so instead buy a big organic chicken that has been allowed to grow slowly from a butcher and ask him to de-bone it and open it out like a book. This is a recipe that takes a bit of work, but it is worth it for a special occasion as the meat is full of beautiful rich flavours in every slice. Serve it with roast potatoes and a green vegetable such as spinach, sautéd in a pan with a little butter and olive oil, and some garlic too, if you like.

(see picture on next page)

1 Preheat the oven to 180°C/gas 4. **2** To make the stuffing, heat a little olive oil in a pan, add the onion and cook gently until soft and translucent. **3** Add the chicken livers, season them and cook until the livers start to caramelise. **4** Add the Marsala and bubble up to evaporate the alcohol, then lift out the livers on to a chopping board and chop finely. Leave to cool. **5** In a large bowl, mix together all the rest of the ingredients for the stuffing and stir in the cooled chicken livers. **6** Lay the chicken skin-side down, season and spoon the stuffing down the centre. **7** Bring the sides of the chicken over the top, then roll it over so that it is breast-side up.

8 Lay the slices of pancetta over the top and then tie up with butcher's string. Tie it lengthways first then crossways, knotting the string every 2cm. **9** Season the chicken all over.

10 Scatter the vegetables, garlic and herbs over the base of a roasting tin. **11** Put in the chicken and drizzle with the olive oil. **12** Roast for 2 hours, pouring over the white wine after 20 minutes, then after that pour a ladleful of chicken stock over the bird every 15 minutes. Keep a little stock back in case you need it to thin the sauce later. **13** To check that the chicken is cooked, insert a skewer into the centre. It should come out hot and the juices should run clear. If you have a thermometer the centre of the meat should be above 60°C. **14** Remove from the oven, lift the chicken on to a large, hot serving plate, and leave to rest for 15 minutes.

15 Meanwhile, transfer the vegetables, herbs and the wine, stock and chicken juices from the roasting tin into a blender and whiz to a sauce consistency, adding a little of the hot stock that you have kept back, if it is too thick. **16** Slice the chicken and spoon the sauce over the top.

Serves 6

chicken 1 large (2.5kg), free-range, preferably organic, de-boned
pancetta 4 slices
carrot 1 large, chopped
celery 1 stalk, chopped
onion 1, chopped
garlic 2 cloves
fresh rosemary 1 sprig
bay leaf 1
olive oil 4 tablespoons
white wine 200ml
good hot chicken stock 2 litres

For the stuffing:
olive oil
onion 1, finely chopped
chicken livers 100g, preferably organic
sea salt and freshly ground black pepper
Marsala 1 glass (70ml)
good pork sausagemeat 400g
vacuum-packed chestnuts 100g (or fresh nuts, roasted as on page 91), finely chopped
dried apricots 60g, soaked in water for 45 minutes–1 hour to plump them up, then finely chopped
dried porcini 50g, soaked in warm water for 3 hours, then finely chopped
white bread 2 slices, soaked in just enough milk to soften
grated Parmesan 2 tablespoons
egg 1
finely chopped fresh rosemary and sage leaves 1 tablespoon, mixed together

Crespelle with sausage, radicchio and ricotta

These make a great weekend lunch, especially as you can make the pancakes in advance, then just fold them around the meat filling and bake them, a bit like tacos.

Radicchio and pork are so special together and the ricotta really combines their flavours. We used to make hundreds of these for the big parties and wedding receptions which were held most weekends at our family's restaurant in Corgeno, La Cinzianella, and I would often be in charge of making the pancakes, hundreds of them, with my uncle Alfio, who was a little dynamo in the kitchen. What a guy; he had so much energy and craft and speed in his hands, you had to be very fast to try to keep up with him.

Later, when I had to do my military service in the army, I told no one that I could cook because I didn't want to end up making massive vats of food all day, but in the first months everyone had to do four or five days of washing up. When I went into the kitchens to do my first shift, there was a guy sweating over the stove trying to make crespelle. The mixture, which had to be made with powdered egg, was too thin and the pancakes weren't working. 'How many do you have to make?' '240...' This guy had managed to do about 20 only. So I made a deal with him: 'Give me two pans and go and get some beers.' I thickened up the mixture, got to work with the two pans and by the time he had been to the store-room and back with the beers, I already had a stack of pancakes ready to go.

1 To make the pancake batter, beat the eggs in a large bowl with the milk. **2** Whisk in the flour slowly, passing it through a fine sieve, to avoid lumps. **3** Put the batter into the fridge for an hour, during which time it will thicken up.

4 To make the filling, heat the olive oil in a large pan, add the onion and cook gently until soft and translucent. **5** Squeeze out the sausagemeat from the casings into the pan and cook for 3–4 minutes. **6** Add the white wine, and bubble up to evaporate the alcohol. **7** Put in the chopped radicchio and cook for another couple of minutes, until it softens, then take off the heat and leave to cool.

Makes 18 crespelle

For the pancakes:

eggs 5	
full-fat milk 500ml	
00 flour 150g	
butter 100g	

8 Stir in the ricotta, Parmesan and chilli. **9** Preheat the oven to 180°C/gas 4.

10 To make the pancakes, grease a non-stick frying pan with a little of the butter over a medium heat and add a small ladleful of the mixture – just enough to cover the base thinly. **11** Cook for 1 minute, until the underside has taken on a light golden colour, then flip over and cook for another 30 seconds. Lift out and repeat with the rest of the mixture, so that you have a stack of 18 pancakes. **12** Spoon some of the sausagemeat mixture on to each pancake – just off centre. **13** Fold the pancake in half over the top of the mixture, and then again into quarters. **14** Line two roasting tins with baking paper and divide the folded pancakes between them.

15 Melt the remaining butter and brush a little over the top of each pancake, then put into the preheated oven for 10 minutes, until the tops become slightly golden and crispy. **16** While the pancakes are in the oven, make the sauce. **17** Bring the cream to just under the boil in a pan, then slowly stir in the Parmesan until it has melted. **18** To serve, spoon the sauce into the base of a warmed serving dish and arrange the pancakes on top. If you like, finish with a little more grated Parmesan.

For the filling:

olive oil 2 tablespoons

onion 1 large, finely chopped

good pork sausages 6

white wine 1 glass (70ml)

radicchio 4, chopped

fresh ricotta 100g

Parmesan 50g, grated

dried chilli 1 teaspoon

sea salt and freshly ground black pepper

For the sauce:

double cream 300ml

Parmesan 120g, grated

To finish:

a little extra grated Parmesan (optional)

Bombetta

I am one of the *fettine* generation of Italians. *Una fetta* is a slice; *una fettine* is a little slice, and when I was growing up, two or three times a week we would have these thin slivers of chicken, of veal, beef or pork, whatever was available from Stefanino the butcher in the village. I don't think I was even aware which meat it was, it was just a *fettine*. At home, or if we went to eat at the house of friends, the mother or grandmother would make some pasta, and then you would be asked, 'Would you like a *fettine* afterwards?' By the time you had finished your pasta, it would be ready. It might be breaded for *milanese* (see page 110), or rolled up around some cheese and ham to make *involtini* (little bundles), pan-fried in butter.

Every area has its own variation. Around Rome, if a slice of veal has a sage leaf added and is rolled up inside a slice of prosciutto it becomes *saltimbocca*, so called because the flavours 'leap in the mouth'. And on holiday in Puglia I first saw *bombetta* in the butcher's shop: similar to *involtini*, but the wrapping meat was *capocollo*: a salumi made with neck of pork which has been cured in a natural casing. When I saw the little skewered parcels on the butcher's counter they immediately said 'home' to me and brought back so many memories of my grandmother's cooking that I wanted to experiment with my own version of a *bombetta* using pork shoulder *fettine* as the wrapping, and this is the recipe. You could wrap the little parcels in an additional layer of *capocollo* over the pork before grilling or barbecuing, if you like. Alternatively you could do as some of the butchers in Puglia do, and roll the parcels in some breadcrumbs mixed with either dried chilli, chopped rosemary, or chopped pistachio nuts, before cooking.

1 Put the steaks in between two sheets of clingfilm and flatten with a meat hammer or the end of a rolling pin until about 3mm thick. **2** Cut each piece into three. **3** Put around a tablespoon of sausagemeat in the centre of each piece. **4** Fold the pork in at each side, to make a little parcel, but try not to overlap too much, just enough to allow you to encase the sausagemeat. **5** Thread two of the parcels onto each of 6 skewers. **6** Barbecue or grill slowly over a low heat for 15–20 minutes or until the sausagemeat is cooked through, but stays soft inside, while the pork wrapping becomes brown and crisp.

Makes 12 skewers
pork shoulder steaks 4
good pork sausagemeat 600g

Pork ribs and cabbage

This is a really simple winter dish. Start it off at 5.30p.m. and after that it cooks itself and by 7.30p.m. you have something fantastic for dinner. Sometimes if I have the end of a salami or some ham in the fridge, I will chop it up and add it to the onions, and I like to just take off the outer leaves from the cabbage, then slice the rest into quarters, so you have nice thick pieces. It will look like a lot of cabbage when it goes into the pan, but it cooks right down to nothing. Serve it with polenta, mashed potato, or baked potatoes with a little knob of butter; delicious.

1 Preheat the oven to 200°C/gas 6. **2** Put the ribs into a roasting pan, season them and put into the preheated oven for 40 minutes until they are dark brown. **3** After the ribs have been in the oven for 10 minutes, heat some olive oil in a large pan, put in the onions and the bay leaves and cook gently until soft and translucent. **4** Add the cabbage, put on the lid and cook gently for 30 minutes. **5** Pour in the white wine, bubble up to evaporate the alcohol, then add the white wine vinegar and finally stir in the tomato purée. Take off the heat. **6** Remove the roasting tin from the oven and turn it down to 170°C/gas 3. **7** Add the contents of the pan of onions and cabbage to the roasting tin, together with the stock, and return to the oven to cook gently for 1½–2 hours, until the meat falls away from the bones.

Serves 4

pork rib racks, 2 whole

sea salt and freshly ground black pepper

olive oil

onions 4, sliced

bay leaves 3

Savoy cabbage 1 large (or 2 small ones), roughly sliced

white wine 50ml

white wine vinegar 100ml

tomato purée 80g

good hot chicken stock 1 litre

Pork belly with chickpeas and turnip tops

We always had bags of chickpeas in the cupboard when Margherita was at home because she could eat almost all pulses, and *cime di rapa* – turnip tops, or turnip greens, as they are often called in the UK – were one of the green vegetables that she could have. Their special broccoli-like flavour goes so well with the pork, but when they are not available, you could substitute chard, or even kale. In this case, the chickpeas are cooked along with the pork absorbing all the flavours during the long cooking, so you really do need to use dried ones, as ready-cooked ones won't stand up so well to two hours in the oven.

1 Soak the chickpeas overnight in cold water. **2** When you are ready to cook, cut the pork belly into six squares. **3** Preheat the oven to 180°C/gas 4. **4** Heat a little olive oil in a casserole dish or pan that will transfer to the oven, put in the pork belly and sear it on each side until golden. **5** Lift out on to a plate and put the pancetta, onions, garlic and rosemary into the casserole. **6** Cook gently until the onion is soft and translucent, then add the chickpeas together with their soaking water (if necessary, add a little more water – just enough to cover). **7** Bring to the boil, cover with a lid, then transfer to the oven for 2 hours. **8** Take the casserole dish from the oven and return it to the hob. The cooking liquid should be quite thick, but if not, lift out the pork belly and bubble it up to reduce it further. **9** Put in the turnip tops and cook for a further 5 minutes. **10** Season well, especially with pepper, and if you have removed the pork belly, return it the casserole, then serve.

Serves 6

dried chickpeas	300g
skinless pork belly	2kg
olive oil	
diced pancetta	50g
white onions	2, chopped
garlic	2 cloves, chopped
fresh rosemary	2 sprigs
turnip tops	300g, chopped
sea salt and freshly ground black pepper	

Braised neck of pork with cannellini beans

Every European culture has a wealth of pork and bean dishes that vary according to the localised production. When we are on holiday in Puglia we go to a restaurant where they have an enormous fireplace with a chimney and they fill up big terracotta jars with different varieties of beans, put in some pieces of vegetables and water, then put the pots next to the fire for about 7–8 hours, so they cook slowly by natural convection. You choose your piece of pork, or whatever meat you like, and they grill it for you and then ladle out the beans . . . such a beautiful thing to do.

If you cook the cannellini beans for this dish yourself they have so much more flavour and texture than the pre-cooked ones in jars or tins. I cannot imagine not having bags of dried beans in the cupboard; they are so much a part of the idea that was passed down by my grandparents' generation, that you might have little or no meat, but if you had a sack of beans, you always had something to eat. Remembering to soak them the night before you want to cook them is just a mindset, and then the cooking is really straightforward. Serve with cabbage, kale, cavolo nero or a leafy chicory, blanched briefly and then sautéd in a little olive oil with some garlic, and a little fresh chilli, if you like.

1 Soak the beans in cold water overnight. **2** Preheat the oven to 180°C/gas 4. **3** Put the pork into a roasting tin, season it and put into the oven for 2 hours, adding the white wine about halfway through cooking and basting the meat every so often. **4** Drain the beans and bring to the boil in plenty of fresh unsalted water, then turn down to a simmer for about 45 minutes until tender. Take off the heat, but leave the beans in their cooking water. **5** In a separate pan, heat some olive oil, put in the onions, pancetta and sage, and cook gently until the onion is soft and translucent. **6** With a slotted spoon, lift three-quarters of the beans from their cooking water and add to the onions and pancetta, then stir in the tomato purée and add enough of the cooking liquid from the beans to cover. Simmer for another 20 minutes.

7 Meanwhile, transfer the remaining beans (with a little of their cooking liquid) to a blender and blend to a purée. **8** Add to the pan. **9** Spoon the beans around the pork in the roasting tin, cover with foil and bake for a further 40 minutes. **10** Put the garlic clove on a chopping board and crush into a paste with the back of a large knife. **11** Put the parsley leaves on top and chop finely, so that the garlic and parsley combine and release their flavours into each other. **12** Lift out the pork on to a chopping board. **13** Spoon the beans into a warm serving dish and sprinkle with the parsley and garlic. **14** Carve the pork and arrange on top.

Serves 6

dried cannellini beans 500g

pork neck 2kg, rolled and tied with string

sea salt and freshly ground black pepper

white wine 1 glass (70ml)

olive oil a little

onions 2 large, finely chopped

diced pancetta 150g

finely chopped fresh sage leaves 2 tablespoons

tomato purée 100g

garlic 1 clove

fresh parsley a handful, finely chopped

Porchetta

Pork belly, spread with herbs and lemon zest, then rolled up and slowly roasted until the meat is sweet and the skin is golden and crispy, is another very traditional thing to have at Christmas in some regions of Italy. It makes a great Sunday lunch with green vegetables and some potatoes roasted in their skins in olive oil, for the last hour of the cooking time for the pork. Sprinkle in some rosemary towards the end of cooking. And any leftover meat makes the best sandwich – around Italy, especially in the region of Lazio outside Rome, they have dedicated porchetta vans which travel to festivals and football matches or park up at the side of the road where they will carve you a thick slice of roasted meat and crackling and hand it to you between fat slices of bread – I would be so happy to be riding around the countryside on the motorbike on a summer's day and then pull over for a porchetta sandwich.

1 Lay the pork skin side down and season with salt. Roughly crush the rest of the ingredients (except the lemon juice and white wine) using a pestle and mortar and spread over the meat, then squeeze the lemon juice over the top. 2 Roll up the pork and tie with string as tightly as possible, making a knot every 2cm, and leave to rest for 1 hour at room temperature to let the garlic and herbs infuse the meat. 3 Preheat the oven to 180°C/gas 4. 4 Cover the base of a roasting tin with a little water (about 5mm deep). 5 Put in the pork, scatter the skin with a little sea salt, then place in the oven for 4 hours, sprinkling in a little of the white wine every half an hour. Then, when the wine is finished, spoon over some of the cooking juices every half an hour. 6 When the pork is done the skin will be golden and crisp and if you insert a skewer into the meat the juices will run clear. 7 Remove from the oven and leave to rest in a warm place for 30 minutes, then carve into thick slices.

Serves 6

pork belly 1 (minus ribs), about 3–4kg

sea salt

black peppercorns 1 teaspoon, crushed

dried chilli 1 teaspoon (optional)

chopped fresh rosemary 1 tablespoon

fennel seeds 1 teaspoon

garlic 2 cloves, finely chopped

lemon zest and juice of 1

white wine 100ml

Lamb shanks with artichokes

The brilliant thing about lamb shanks is that they are virtually impossible to overcook, as long as you do it really gently – a slow cooker is great for this. The meat will be meltingly tender and will just fall away from the bone. I suggest one small shank per person for a main course, but if I was cooking for six and serving some antipasti and then a little risotto or pasta, I would just cook three shanks. They would be enough to put in the middle of the table, with a bowl of soft polenta or mashed potatoes, and let everyone help themselves.

Out of the artichoke season, this is good with some balsamic vinegar – just a dash stirred into the sauce halfway through the cooking time in the oven can give it a real lift. Then, if you like, right at the end, you can whisk in a little more balsamic vinegar and a knob of butter before serving.

1 Prepare the artichokes as on page 63 and cut in half. **2** Preheat the oven to 180°C/gas 4. **3** Have the flour ready in a shallow bowl. **4** Season the lamb shanks, then dust with the flour. **5** Heat half the oil in a large casserole dish or pan that will transfer to the oven, put in the shanks and colour on all sides. **6** Lift out, add the onions and cook gently until soft and translucent, then add the bottle of red wine, bubble up to evaporate the alcohol, and continue to simmer until the liquid has reduced by half. **7** Add 2 litres of the stock, the tomato purée, and the bouquet garni, return the shanks to the pan, bring back to the boil, then turn down the heat, cover with a lid and transfer to the preheated oven for 2½–3 hours, until the meat is tender and falls away from the bones.

8 Meanwhile, heat the rest of the oil in a pan, add the crushed clove of garlic and the bay leaf and sauté until the garlic is golden but not burnt. **9** Add the artichokes and season. **10** Pour in the white wine and, as before, bubble up to allow the alcohol to evaporate, then add the rest of the chicken stock. Bring back to the boil, then turn down to a simmer for 5 minutes. **11** Take off the heat and remove the garlic and bay leaf.

12 Remove the casserole from the oven and carefully lift the meat out of the cooking liquid on to a warm plate. Discard the bouquet garni, then put the casserole on the hob and bubble up the liquid to reduce it to a sauce consistency. **13** Put the lamb back in, together with the contents of the pan of artichokes, let everything heat through, then serve, drizzled with extra virgin olive oil.

Serves 6

globe artichokes 6 small

plain flour 4 tablespoons

lamb shanks 6 small

sea salt and freshly ground black pepper

olive oil 4 tablespoons

onions 2, finely chopped

full-bodied red wine 1 bottle

chicken (or lamb) stock 3 litres

tomato purée 1 tablespoon

bouquet garni 1, made with 1 sprig of fresh rosemary, 5 fresh sage leaves, 2 bay leaves and 1 clove of garlic, tied inside a piece of muslin

garlic 1 whole clove, lightly crushed

bay leaf 1

white wine 100ml

extra virgin olive oil to serve

Leg of lamb with peppers and mint

This is a very colourful, spring-like way to roast lamb. Red wine gives a great depth of flavour, but you could use white wine if you prefer, and some extra chopped fresh mint scattered over just before carving really heightens the fresh sweetness of the peppers and the meat. Serve it simply with some roast potatoes.

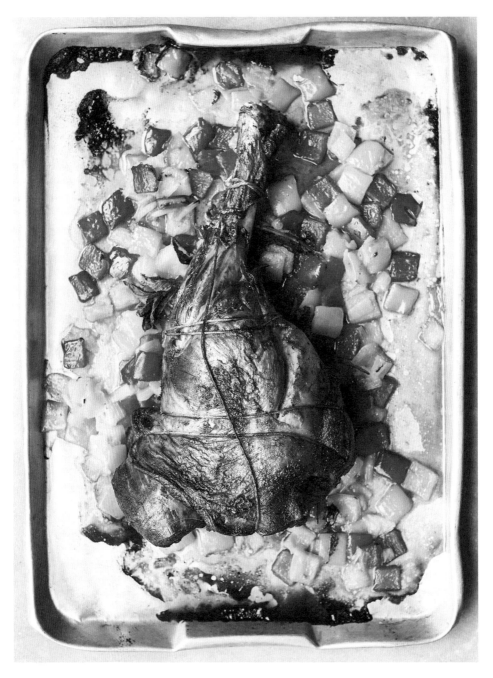

1 Preheat the oven to 180°C/gas 4. **2** Chop 2 of the garlic cloves finely with half the mint leaves. **3** With a sharp knife make 10–12 deep slits into the lamb, then push a teaspoon of the garlic and mint mixture inside. **4** Heat the olive oil in a roasting tin on the hob, then season the lamb and colour on both sides. **5** Add half the chopped onions along with the carrot, celery, the remaining whole garlic clove and the rosemary and cook until the vegetables begin to colour, taking care not to burn the garlic. **6** Add half the red wine and bubble up to evaporate the alcohol, then transfer the tin to the oven. Allow to cook for 20 minutes, then add the rest of the wine and cook for another 5 minutes. **7** Now add half the stock and then leave in the oven for a further 20 minutes. This will give you medium-cooked meat, depending on the size of the leg, so if necessary, or you prefer the meat more well done, leave it in the oven for a little longer.

8 When the meat is ready, take the roasting tin from the oven, and lift out the meat while you discard the rosemary and the whole clove of garlic, then pour the contents of the roasting tin into a blender. **9** Return the lamb to the tin, add the peppers with the rest of the onions, season, add a ladleful of the remaining stock and put back in the oven for another 10 minutes until the peppers are cooked but still crunchy. **10** Meanwhile, put a few of the remaining mint leaves (around 10) into the blender and blend, adding as much of the rest of the stock as necessary to produce a sauce consistency. **11** Transfer this to a small pan and keep warm on the hob.

12 Remove the lamb from the oven and leave to rest for 15 minutes before carving. **13** Lift out the peppers to a warm serving dish and stir in the rest of the mint leaves. **14** Carve the lamb and lay the slices on top. Serve with the sauce on the side.

Serves 6

garlic 3 cloves

fresh mint 1 large bunch, leaves only

leg of lamb 1

olive oil 2 tablespoons

sea salt and freshly ground black pepper

onions 2 large, chopped

carrot 1, chopped

celery 1 stalk, chopped

fresh rosemary 2 sprigs

red wine 2 glasses (150ml)

chicken stock 2 litres

peppers 4 yellow and 4 red, preferably long Romano, deseeded and roughly chopped

Slow-cooked shoulder of lamb with anchovy sauce

When you cook lamb shoulder slowly, slowly over about four hours, the meat is unbelievably tender and juicy and will almost fall off the bone. In Dubai and throughout the Middle East and North Africa it is a very old idea to slow-cook lamb like this, with different spices in all kinds of ovens, but essentially the idea is the same: to tenderise the meat from even an old animal. Then it is usually shredded and mixed with the cooking juices on top of a big pot of rice in the middle of the table, so everyone can pull off some of the tender meat and spoon out some rice: and it is really delicious.

1 Preheat the oven to 160°C/gas 3. **2** Heat the olive oil in a large roasting tin on the hob. **3** Season the meat, put it into the tin and colour on all sides, add the wine and bubble up to evaporate the alcohol, then add a wine glass (70ml) of water. **4** Take off the heat, cover the pan with foil and transfer to the oven for 4 hours, until the lamb is very tender. **5** Put the anchovies into a blender and start to blend, adding the vegetable oil very slowly, together with a few tablespoons of warm water as necessary to give a creamy sauce. **6** Remove the meat from the bones (it will fall away easily) and cut into rough slices. **7** Arrange on a warm serving dish. **8** In a bowl quickly toss the salad leaves with the dressing. **9** Serve the lamb with the salad and the sauce on the side.

Serves 6

olive oil 4 tablespoons

sea salt and freshly ground black pepper

shoulder of lamb 1

white wine 1 glass (70ml)

good anchovy fillets in oil 200g, drained

vegetable oil 100ml

mixed salad leaves

Giorgio's dressing 100ml (see page 19)

Osso buco

I have never put osso buco on the menu at Locanda, but I thought that if I didn't include a recipe for it in this book, I would be a traitor to my heritage, as it was so much a part of our family eating when I was growing up. My grandmother made it, not with veal calves raised in the cruel crate system that was finally outlawed in the UK in 1990, and in Europe in 2007, but with local mountain calves that wandered free.

I have often made osso buco at home in London with rose veal, because Margherita could eat everything that goes into the pan. It is a really simple recipe that is all about the flavour from the veal shin bones. Osso buco means 'bone with a hole', or 'hollow bones', and it is the marrow inside this hollow that makes the meat so unctuous and delicious when you cook it slowly over a few hours. Right at the end, you add the big kick of flavour that comes from the gremolata: lemon zest, chopped parsley and garlic, which will always liven up any stew.

In our family we would always serve osso buco in the traditional Milanese way with saffron risotto (see page 182), which you can start to make about twenty minutes before the meat is ready.

1 Have the flour ready in a shallow bowl. **2** Season the shins and then dust them in the flour. **3** Heat the oil in a large pan, add the shins and sauté until golden on both sides. **4** Lift them out to a plate, then put all the vegetables into the pan and sauté for 3–4 minutes, until the onions are soft and translucent. **5** Add the white wine and bubble up to evaporate, then stir in the tomato purée and return the shins to the pan. **6** Pour in the stock, put in the bouquet garni, bring to the boil, then turn down the heat, cover with a lid and cook very, very slowly for 2½ hours.

7 Lift out the shins and bubble up the liquid in the pan to reduce it to a sauce consistency. **8** Transfer to a warmed serving dish. **9** Mix the lemon zest, parsley and garlic together for the gremolata and sprinkle on top. Remind everyone to prise out all the marrow from the bones with a knife.

Serves 6

plain flour 4 tablespoons

sea salt and freshly ground black pepper

rose veal shin bones 6, around 4–5cm thick

olive oil 4 tablespoons

onions 2, finely chopped

carrots 2, finely chopped

celery 2 stalks, finely chopped

white wine 1 glass (70ml)

tomato purée 1 tablespoon

good beef stock 3 litres

bouquet garni 1, made with 1 sprig of fresh rosemary, 5 fresh sage leaves, 2 bay leaves and 1 clove of garlic tied inside a piece of muslin

For the gremolata:

lemons zest of 2

fresh parsley a small bunch, finely chopped

garlic 2 cloves, finely chopped

The Tuesday burger

When chefs and waiters who used to work at Locanda drop around to see us it always seems to be around 4.30p.m. on a Tuesday or a Saturday. Why? Because they know that on Saturday the staff meal is pizza (pages 184-87) and on Tuesday we make the burgers, and they are too good to miss.

The reputation of the burger has suffered very badly in our commercial food culture that so often strips the goodness out of our food, and then convinces people that this is what they want to eat. A well-made burger can be completely delicious, and at home I took the view that the way to try to convince Margherita and Jack not to eat cheap processed burgers was to show them how to make better, homemade ones.

Staff burger night is the only time we allow ketchup in the kitchen at Locanda; and sometimes we forget to order it, so we have to run downstairs and borrow some from the hotel kitchens. Of course you can add anything you like to the burgers, but we keep ours quite simple. We just add a bit of an Italian flavour with caciocavallo cheese, which is made in the south of the country and in Sicily. The name, which means 'cheese on horseback', is said to come from the fact that the stretched curd (*pasta filata*) is formed in little round pouches which used to be strung up in pairs, like saddle-bags, over beams in the cheesemakers' cellars. It is quite a strong and spicy cheese, but if you prefer you could put in some milder mozzarella, which comes from the same *pasta filata* family. I love a thick slice of pickled gherkin, the kind that you see in fish and chip shops, but the other Italians at the restaurant don't like that. In Italy we don't have those big gherkins and so every time we put them in the burgers, the guys would pull them out again straight away.

One of the things that makes the burgers so good is the quality of the buns, which we make ourselves in the kitchen. I am not saying that you have to do the same, though I have given a recipe opposite, and if you have the time, it is a lovely thing to do. But if you don't have time, try to buy good ones. When you make burgers or any kind of sandwich, remember that you can use the best ingredients but then spoil the whole experience by surrounding them with bad bread.

Any time you make a mixture for burgers, *involtini*, or a stuffing for ravioli, if you are not binding it with egg, it is always best to let it rest for as long as you can before shaping it, so that it will hold together and not break up.

(see picture on next page)

1 In a bowl mix the flour, yeast, sugar, melted butter and salt with 300ml water at room temperature until you have a dough. **2** Divide it into six and roll into balls. **3** Cover with clingfilm and leave to prove for 3 hours until doubled in size.

4 Heat a little olive oil in a pan and add the onion. **5** Sauté gently until soft and translucent, then take the pan from the heat and leave to cool.

6 Preheat the oven to 200°C/gas 6. **7** Line a baking tray with baking paper and place the balls of dough on top. Brush the tops with beaten egg and sprinkle with sesame seeds, then bake in the preheated oven for 20 minutes, until the buns are light golden on top and the bases sound hollow when tapped. **8** Take out of the oven and leave to cool while you make the burgers, but leave the oven on.

9 In a large bowl mix the cooled, sautéd onion with the rest of the burger ingredients, adding the seasoning right at the end. **10** Let the mixture rest in the fridge, for at least 20 minutes, but a couple of hours is better, so that it will fuse together and won't break up when you shape the meat into six patties. **11** Preheat a grill to hot. **12** Heat the vegetable oil in a sauté pan that will transfer to the oven. **13** Pan-fry the patties on both sides until they form a golden brown crust, then put into the oven for about 5 minutes for medium-rare meat, or longer if you prefer.

14 While the burgers are in the oven, split each bun and toast the cut sides quickly under the hot grill until dark golden. **15** Spoon a little ketchup and mayonnaise on to each base, add a burger and top with cheese, then a slice of tomato. Sprinkle this with salt and a little oregano, add some red onion and a slice of gherkin, if you like. **16** Finish with a lettuce leaf and put the top on the bun.

Makes 6 burgers

For the buns:

00 flour 600g	
fresh yeast 10g	
sugar 60g	
melted butter 40g	
fine sea salt 15g	
egg 1, beaten	
sesame seeds 1 tablespoon	

For the burgers:

olive oil	
onion 1, finely chopped	
minced beef 750g, medium-ground	
Worcestershire sauce 2 tablespoons	
Tabasco sauce 1 tablespoon	
finely chopped rosemary and sage leaves 1 tablespoon, mixed together	
eggs 2	
sea salt and freshly ground black pepper	
vegetable oil 1 tablespoon, for frying	

To garnish:

tomato ketchup 2 tablespoons	
good mayonnaise 2 tablespoons	
caciocavallo cheese or good cow's milk mozzarella 6 slices	
tomatoes 2 large, each sliced into three	
dried oregano a pinch	
red onion 1, thinly sliced	
gherkins 2 large, sliced (optional)	
Cos or Romaine lettuce leaves 6	

Beef stew with peas and potatoes

When Plaxy and I were on holiday in Puglia we were taken by a friend to a tiny local restaurant where the wife cooks and the husband serves, the wine is a simply a choice between red or white, and the bill is the equivalent of about £15 if you are with someone local, £20 otherwise. Our friend asked for *spezzatino* (stew), so I said, 'I'll have that too,' and out it came, made with beef from the leg or shoulder and whole big potatoes, served in a bowl with a piece of bread, and it was exactly like the *spezzatino* that my grandmother used to make. When I tasted it, it was as if I was 4 foot tall again, sitting at the table eating it with my brother when we came home from school.

At home in London when we made this stew, we always put in peas for Margherita, and it was something we could have cooking gently all day in the slow cooker and it would be ready for her and Jack to have in the evening. Like all stews of this kind, it is even better if you put any that is left over into the fridge and reheat it the next day.

1 Preheat the oven to 160°C/gas 3. **2** Have the flour ready in a shallow bowl. **3** Heat the olive oil in a casserole dish that will transfer to the oven. **4** Season the beef, dust it in the flour, then put it into the pan and colour on all sides over quite a high heat. **5** Lift out the meat on to a warm plate, then turn down the heat, put the onion, carrot and celery into the pan and cook for a few minutes, until the onion is soft and translucent. **6** Return the meat to the casserole, stir in the tomato purée, cook for another 3 minutes, then add the wine and bubble up until the liquid has reduced by half. **7** Pour in 2 litres of the stock, add the bouquet garni and bring to the boil. **8** Take off the heat, put on the lid and transfer to the oven for 45 minutes. **9** Add the potatoes to the casserole and cook for another 30 minutes, adding more hot stock as necessary, as the potatoes will absorb some of the liquid. **10** Finally add the peas and cook for another 10 minutes. **11** Remove the bouquet garni, and taste and season again if necessary before serving.

Serves 6

plain flour 3 tablespoons	
olive oil 4 tablespoons	
sea salt and freshly ground black pepper	
diced beef (such as shoulder) 2kg	
onion 1, chopped	
carrot 1, chopped	
celery 1 stalk, chopped	
tomato purée 1 tablespoon	
full-bodied red wine 2 glasses (150ml)	
good hot beef stock 3 litres	
bouquet garni 1, made with 1 sprig of fresh rosemary, 5 fresh sage leaves, 2 bay leaves and 1 clove of garlic, tied inside a piece of muslin	
potatoes 5 medium, quartered	
fresh shelled peas 400g (or frozen peas, defrosted under running water)	

Polenta
x 4

If I were to look in the store cupboard at home and see no polenta (cornmeal), that would be a minor disaster, not only for me but for Margherita, because it was one of the things she could eat freely.

In the days when people rarely travelled far beyond their region, southern Italians called us northerners *polentone*, because they said we ate polenta all the time, which wasn't true: we ate rice all the time. But we did eat a lot of it, with stews or with rabbit, or sometimes the soft polenta would be baked (*polenta concia*), layered up with lots of cheese, and sometimes ragù. On a Sunday when the family was all together in Corgeno, my dad would make the polenta in a big copper pot over the wood-fired stove that my grandad built in the garden and often friends and neighbours would join us. That polenta is locked into my sense of the celebration of people coming together to eat, because he elevated it into something special. For almost an hour he would be in the garden tending the pot with the big wooden stirrer that my grandad had also made and the polenta would take on an almost smoky taste from the wood fire. When it was done he would turn it out like a massive cake and we would eat it with my mum's pork or beef ragù.

As kids we would wet our hands, then, once it was cool enough to touch, take little pieces of polenta, roll them into balls and push a little piece of Gorgonzola inside, which would melt in the heat. We would eat *la camicia*, 'the shirt', which was the crusty bit left around the inside of the pot, at the end of the meal with a little bit of sugar sprinkled over it. And if there was any polenta left over it was allowed to set, and then the next day it was grilled.

The polenta we use is *bramata*, from *bramapura*, which means stone-milled, and it is medium ground, a little coarse in texture, sometimes with little specks of husk. It can be white (ground from white varieties of corn) or golden. I am not keen on fast-cook polenta, as the grains don't hold the same strength, and the cooked polenta has a different, emasculated texture.

Each recipe overleaf makes enough for 6.

With Gorgonzola and radicchio

This is classic, soft creamy polenta that goes so well with meat stews or a ragù of pork or beef.

1 In a pan bring 1.6 litres of milk to the boil with 400ml of double cream and 20g of salt. **2** Slowly whisk in 230g of polenta and keep stirring over a low heat. **3** After about 5 minutes it will start to thicken. Keep stirring for another 30 minutes. The polenta is ready when it comes away easily from the sides of the pan. Take off the heat and keep warm. **4** Halve 3 heads of radicchio tardivo, sprinkle with sea salt, freshly ground black pepper and drizzle with a little extra virgin olive oil, then put under a medium grill until the stems are tender and the leaves take on some colour. **5** Stir 2 tablespoons of Gorgonzola into the polenta until it has completely melted in. **6** Transfer to a warm serving dish. **7** Crumble over 2 more tablespoons of Gorgonzola and put the grilled radicchio on the side.

Baked polenta 'gnocchi'

Gnocchi is simply a word for dumplings, in this case made with polenta and cheese. These are also fantastic with meat stews.

1 Make the polenta in the same way as the recipe above, but use 400ml of milk, 100ml of double cream, 5g of salt and 60g of polenta. **2** Take off the heat and cool to room temperature, then stir in 180g of 00 flour and 2 egg yolks and mix into a firm dough. **3** Preheat the oven to 180°C/gas 4. **4** Take pieces of the polenta and roll them gently into balls (the size of a golf ball). **5** Bring a large pan of salted water to the boil, turn off the heat, put in the balls of polenta and cook for 3 minutes – in batches if necessary – then drain well. **6** Brush a roasting tin with a little melted butter and put in the balls of polenta. **7** Sprinkle around 3 tablespoons of grated Parmesan over the top and put into the preheated oven for 10–15 minutes, until the cheese has melted and forms a golden crust.

Grilled

In Italy people will still often just turn out a pan of polenta on to a chopping board, wait just long enough for it not to scald their hands, then shape it into a rough oblong shape, as it will start to solidify quite quickly. Then, once it is hard, they will slice it into squares or oblongs with a cheese wire. However, it is easier on your hands if you let it solidify in a tin. This needs to be a firmer polenta than for the recipe opposite, made with water instead of cream and milk. These are good served with *bagna cauda* or a cheese dip or just dusted with grated Parmesan.

1 Bring 600ml of water to the boil in a pan. **2** Slowly whisk in 200g of polenta and a pinch of sea salt. Keep stirring over a low heat. After about 5 minutes it will start to thicken. Keep stirring for another 45 minutes. It is ready when it comes away easily from the sides of the pan. **3** Brush a loaf tin with olive oil. **4** Take the pan off the heat, pour in the polenta and leave until it is solid. **5** Now you can turn the polenta out on to a board or clean work surface. Cut it into slices about 1cm thick and then again into wedges. **6** Grill the slices on both sides until golden and crisp (or pan-fry on both sides in a non-stick pan, just rubbed with a tiny bit of olive oil).

Polenta crisps

We made these for Margherita as an alternative to the rice crisps on pages 124-25, which she couldn't have, because until recently she was allergic to rice.

1 Bring 250ml of water to the boil, then whisk in 60g of polenta and 4g of fine sea salt and keep stirring for 45 minutes until it is smooth and gluey. Then blend it to smooth out any lumps. An easier alternative is to make it in a Thermomix, or similar multi-skill food processor that cooks as well as chops and mixes. Just pour the water into the bowl and set the temperature to 100°C. When it reaches that point, add the polenta and salt and leave to cook for 45 minutes. Either way, while the polenta is still warm, spread it with a spatula as thinly as possible over a large sheet of greaseproof paper and leave (preferably overnight) until cool and completely dried out. You should be able to lift the polenta easily from the paper without it sticking.
2 Heat some vegetable oil to 180°C in a deep-fryer or a large pan (no more than a third full). If you don't have a thermometer, drop in some flour and it should start to sizzle gently. **3** Break the polenta into shards and deep-fry in batches. As soon as the pieces puff and crisp up, lift them out with a slotted spoon and drain on kitchen paper.

Char-grilled quail with apple, frisée and lamb's lettuce

This is a really fresh salad with some nice acidity and sharpness from the apple. In summer you can grill the quail on the barbecue, if you like, and if you want to put a bit of time and effort into making this a quite special dish, you could pair it with the quail and chicken liver crostini on page 115.

1 With kitchen scissors, cut each quail in half. **2** Put into a large dish or container and scatter with the slices of garlic and chilli, add the rosemary and drizzle with half the olive oil. Leave in the fridge to marinate for 12 hours, or overnight. **3** When ready to cook, lift the quail from the marinade and pat them dry with kitchen paper. **4** Preheat the oven to 180°C/gas 4. **5** Heat a griddle pan or sauté pan that will transfer to the oven and cook the halves of quail, skin side down, until the skin is crispy. **6** Transfer the pan to the oven for 3–4 minutes, until the quail meat is cooked through. To check, insert a sharp knife into the thighs and the juices should run clear. **7** In a large bowl mix the lamb's lettuce, frisée and apple and toss with Giorgio's dressing, then transfer to a serving dish, place the quail on top, and finish with the rest of the olive oil and the balsamic vinegar.

Serves 6

quails 6 large

garlic 1 clove, sliced

mild red chilli 1, sliced

fresh rosemary 1 sprig

extra virgin olive oil 4 tablespoons

lamb's lettuce 600g

frisée leaves 2 heads

Granny Smith apples 2, peeled, cored and sliced

Giorgio's dressing 4 tablespoons (see page 20)

apple balsamic (or balsamic) vinegar 3 tablespoons

Roast pigeon with lentils and radicchio

I love pigeon. It reminds me of autumn at home in Lombardy when the hunters would be out in the woods shooting game. Lentils and radicchio done in this way are also good with *cotechino*, the fat pork sausage that is traditional for New Year's Eve and needs to be simmered for around two hours before slicing and serving on top of the lentils. This is one of the 'lucky dishes' that so many cultures have: it is said that if you start the new year with a dish of lentils which are shaped like coins, it will bring you good fortune.

The lentils we use are the ones from Castelluccio, in Umbria, which are small and brown and less starchy than some varieties, so although they become beautifully tender, they hold their shape well. If you can't find them, you can use Puy lentils.

1 Preheat the oven to 180°C/gas 4. **2** Heat the olive oil in a large pan. **3** Add the chopped vegetables and cook gently until just soft, then add the lentils and stir around for a couple of minutes. **4** Add the stock and the bouquet garni, bring to the boil, then turn down to a simmer for 30 minutes until the lentils are tender. **5** Add the radicchio and cook for another 3 minutes, then turn off the heat, taste and season. **6** While the lentils are cooking, season the pigeons inside and out, put into a roasting tray and cook in the preheated oven for 15–20 minutes, until the skin is golden and the juices run clear if you insert a skewer into the thighs. **7** Lift out of the oven, remove the string, and leave to rest for 5–10 minutes.

8 For the garnish, heat half the butter in a sauté pan until it starts to turn slightly brown, put in the sage leaves and toss in the butter until crispy. **9** Lift out and drain on kitchen paper. **10** Put the garlic clove on a chopping board and, with the back of a large knife, crush into a paste. **11** Put the parsley leaves on the top and chop finely, so that the garlic and parsley combine and release their flavours into each other, then stir into the lentils along with the rest of the butter. **12** Transfer to a warmed serving dish. **13** Carve the breasts and legs from each pigeon and arrange on top, then scatter with the sage leaves.

Serves 6

olive oil 2 tablespoons

onion 1, finely chopped

carrot 1, finely chopped

celery 1 stalk, finely chopped

Castelluccio lentils 600g, or other small brown lentils, such as Puy

good chicken stock 2 litres

bouquet garni 1, made with 1 bay leaf, 5 sage leaves, 1 sprig of fresh rosemary and 1 clove of garlic, tied inside a piece of muslin

Chioggia radicchio 1 head

sea salt and freshly ground black pepper

squab pigeons 6, oven-ready

butter 200g

fresh sage leaves a handful

garlic 1 clove

fresh flat-leaf parsley a small bunch, leaves only

Rabbit fricassee

This is a dish full of umami flavours from the dried porcini. We always have a jar of them in the cupboard ready to soak, for a dish like this or to chop into a pan of other mushrooms, as they really help to sustain the flavour of fresh mushrooms without over-powering them. I used to go up into the woods behind our house in Corgeno with my grandad in the autumn searching for porcini – if we found any we would eat some, and then he would lay the rest outside on wooden slats until completely dry for the store cupboard. If you have some wild mushrooms you could add them to this fricassee at the end, after you have reduced the sauce.

This is good with creamy polenta (see page 262) and some chunks of roast courgette and red pepper.

1 Soak the dried porcini in warm water for about 2 hours, until soft, then discard the water, chop and keep to one side. **2** Heat a little olive oil in a large pan, then season the rabbit and put it into the pan. **3** Sauté until it is golden brown on all sides, then lift out on to a warmed plate. **4** Put the onions, pancetta and chopped mushrooms into the pan and cook gently until the onions are soft and translucent, then put the pieces of rabbit back in, add the white wine and bubble up to evaporate the alcohol and reduce the liquid by half. **5** Add the chicken stock, which should completely cover the rabbit.

6 Cover the pan with a lid and cook gently for 1 hour. Some of the pieces may cook through and become tender faster than others, so check the shoulder pieces first and if necessary remove them and keep them warm on a serving dish. **7** When all the pieces are ready, lift them out and add to the dish. If necessary bubble up the sauce in the pan to reduce a little bit, then pour over the rabbit and finish with the lemon zest.

Serves 6

dried porcini mushrooms 50g

olive oil

sea salt and freshly ground black pepper

rabbit 1, cleaned and cut into 10 pieces

onions 2, chopped

diced pancetta 100g

white wine 100ml

good chicken stock 2 litres

lemon grated zest of 1

269

At the end of a meal I prefer some fresh fruit and a little cheese to a dessert, but I have to admit to that very Italian penchant for a slice of homemade cake with a cappuccino mid-morning.

Cakes, treats and ice creams

Lemon and pistachio polenta cake

Obviously I love this cake since I am a *polentone* – a polenta-eater, as southern Italians like to call those of us who come from the north. The polenta, combined with the ground almonds, gives the cake a great texture, but actually the flavours shout to me of the south, since we use the knobbly Amalfi lemons that are very juicy and not as sharp as other varieties, and creamy, bright green pistachios from Bronte in Sicily. Of course you can use any pistachios, but try to avoid hard, dry ones. Any variety of lemon is also fine, and the cake is also good made with limes, or half lemon and half lime. The syrup which coats it is a little like that of an English lemon drizzle cake, but it should be really citrusy, so don't be shy with the lemon (or lime) juice.

I would have loved to bake this for my grandmother and my grandad, because they would never have had a polenta cake. They were of that generation that associated polenta with hard times during the war, when there was little else to eat, and they would not have believed the way subsequent generations have elevated it and in this case used it to create something quite sumptuous.

Of course, neither would they have believed the amount of sugar we now consume as a society, and we need to correct that. But the sugar we should demonise is the hidden quantity in the packets and bottles and cans of processed food we buy and that we cannot control; not the sugar that goes into a cake made at home with beautiful fresh eggs, olive oil or good butter, patience and love.

1 Grease a 24cm round cake tin (about 8cm deep) with a little butter and line with baking paper. **2** Preheat the oven to 160°C/gas 3. **3** Spread the pistachio nuts over a baking tray and put into the preheated oven for 8 minutes, shaking the tray from time to time so that the nuts are golden all over. **4** Remove from the oven and leave to cool. Leave the oven on. **5** In a bowl, cream the butter, sugar, vanilla seeds and lemon zest until pale and fluffy. **6** Fold in the eggs slowly, one at a time, making sure each one is incorporated before adding the next one. **7** Mix the ground almonds, polenta and baking powder in a separate bowl and then fold into the mixture. **8** Finally fold in the roasted pistachio nuts and let the mixture rest for about 10 minutes, so that it absorbs all the ingredients and textures. **9** Spoon into the cake tin and bake in the preheated oven for 1 hour, until the cake is springy to the touch. **10** Just before you take the cake from the oven, whisk the sugar and lemon juice together until the sugar has dissolved. **11** Remove the tin from the oven to a wire rack. **12** While still hot, spoon the glaze over the top of the cake, and leave to cool down before removing it from the tin.

Makes 1 x 24cm cake

pistachio nuts 60g

unsalted butter 230g, softened, plus a little extra for greasing the tin

light demerara sugar 230g

vanilla seeds from 1 pod

unwaxed lemons, preferably Amalfi, zest of 4

eggs 4

ground almonds 230g

polenta 175g

baking powder 2 teaspoons

For the glaze:

caster sugar 150g

lemons juice of the 4 above

Carrot cake

This recipe has a real generosity of carrot flavour. Plaxy used to make it with a passionfruit frosting and put a slice in Jack's lunchbox, or have it ready for him when he came home from school, and the addition of pineapple was one of her tricks to add sweetness without more sugar. Remember that different varieties of carrots are sweeter than others, and they also have their seasons, so when they are fully mature, their natural sugars will be at their peak.

Also, all carrots will sweeten when they cook, so if you taste them when they are raw and they are very sweet you could even increase the quantity and reduce the sugar a little more without upsetting the texture of the cake.

The way you grate the carrots makes a difference, so I would say if you are making the cake to have with a cup of tea in the afternoon then grate them quite chunkily, but if you are making it as an after-dinner cake and piping the frosting to make it look elegant, you might prefer the more refined texture that comes from finer grating.

1 Preheat the oven to 160°C/gas 3. **2** Prepare a 27cm deep round cake tin, with a removable base: grease it with a little butter, tip in some plain flour and swirl it around to dust all over the base and sides, then tip out the excess. **3** In a large bowl, mix the sugar with the eggs and the two oils. **4** Mix together the flour, baking powder, bicarbonate of soda, ground ginger, cinnamon and vanilla seeds, then fold into the sugar, egg and oil mixture. **5** Finally fold in the carrots, all the nuts and the pineapple. **6** Spoon the mixture into the prepared cake tin and smooth the top. **7** Put into the preheated oven and bake for 1 hour, or until a skewer inserted into the centre comes out clean. **8** Remove from the oven and turn out onto a wire rack.

Makes 1 x 27cm round cake

butter and plain flour a little, to prepare the tin

demerara sugar 225g

eggs 3

sunflower oil 160ml

olive oil 65ml, preferably a light-flavoured one

plain flour 225g

baking powder 1 teaspoon

bicarbonate of soda 1 teaspoon

ground ginger a pinch

ground cinnamon 10g

vanilla seeds from 1 pod

carrots 160g, grated

pecan nuts 30g, finely chopped

pistachio nuts 30g, finely chopped

walnuts 30g, finely chopped

fresh pineapple 65g, finely chopped

9 To make the syrup, put the sugar into a pan with 100ml of water and bring to the boil for just long enough for the sugar to dissolve and give a pale syrup. **10** Take off the heat and leave to cool.

11 To make the frosting, beat the butter with half the icing sugar in a bowl until creamy. **12** Add the rest of the icing sugar and the mascarpone and carry on beating until they are incorporated. **13** Mix in the lemon zest. **14** Leave to set in the fridge for about 30 minutes.

15 When cool cut the cake in half horizontally and brush each half with some syrup. **16** Spread half the frosting on to the base layer with a palette knife, then reassemble. **17** Brush the top of the cake with the rest of the syrup and cover with the rest of the frosting. **18** Decorate, if you like, with pumpkin seeds and orange zest.

For the syrup:
caster sugar 100g

For the mascarpone and lemon cream frosting:
unsalted butter 65g, softened
icing sugar 165g
mascarpone 100g
lemon zest of 1

To garnish:
pumpkin seeds (optional)
orange zest cut into thin strips (optional)

Rose bun cake

The name of this comes not from the flavour but from its appearance. The yeasty dough is rolled out, spread with vanilla cream, then rolled up and cut into slices which are arranged tightly in circles in a tin, and when baked they puff up and join together, so that they look like a posy of roses.

1 Grease a deep 26cm round cake tin, with a removable base, with a little butter and line with baking paper. **2** In a bowl mix the milk and the yeast until the yeast has dissolved. **3** Mix in the flour, sugar, oil, egg yolks, salt and lemon zest, then knead by hand into a dough. **4** Leave to rest for 30 minutes, covered with a clean tea towel. **5** Lay a sheet of baking paper on your work surface, put the dough on top, and roll it out into a rectangle about 70cm x 40cm. **6** Leave for another 15 minutes, again covered with a clean tea towel.

7 For the filling, cream the butter, sugar and vanilla seeds together until pale and fluffy. **8** Spread over the dough. **9** Lifting the baking paper to help you, roll it up like a Swiss roll, then slice into 11 pieces. **10** Arrange 8 of the slices around the outside of the cake tin, cut side upwards, and place the final 3 in the middle. **11** Leave to rest in the tin, covered with clingfilm, for 1½ hours, until the 'roses' have risen and joined together.

12 Meanwhile, preheat the oven to 180°C/gas 4. **13** Put the tin into the oven for 30 minutes until golden. **14** Lift out the cake on to a wire rack and leave to cool, then dust with icing sugar. The cake will break into individual 'roses' for serving.

Makes 11 buns

butter, a little, for greasing the tin

full-fat milk 150ml, at room temperature

fresh yeast 25g

00 flour 450g

caster sugar 80g

extra virgin olive oil 2 tablespoons

egg yolks 3

fine salt 1 teaspoon

lemon zest of 1

For the cream filling:

unsalted butter 150g, softened and cut into cubes

caster sugar 150g

vanilla seeds from 1 pod

To finish:

icing sugar for dusting

Paradise cake

This is one of those lovely, soft, light Genoese-style cakes that at one time everyone baked at home. My grandmother used to keep a box on top of the cupboard in our kitchen that sat next to the saffron and was decorated with angels holding a cake. Inside were lots of packets of *Lievito Pane degli Angeli*, baking powder enhanced with vanilla, which is something every Italian family knows. Paradise cake was the only one my grandmother and my mum ever made, apart from a variation which contained raisins, and whenever I asked what was in the packets, my grandmother would say, 'It is what makes the cake really good.' I suppose it made sense to me that angels would be in charge of paradise cake – Italians always like to believe in miracles. I was so fascinated by the packets that one day I climbed up to taste the powder inside, which of course was disappointingly horrible.

The history of the cake is also much more down to earth, as there are all kinds of recipes for it dating back to at least the end of the nineteenth century. However, the most popular story is that it was first made by a monk at a monastery in Pavia, in my region of Lombardy. It is also said that it was a favourite of the opera singer Maria Callas, who used to bake it at her villa alongside Lake Garda.

If you are having a soup or a light meal in the evening, a slice of this makes a good dessert with some fresh fruit.

1 Grease an 18cm round cake tin, with a removable base, with a little butter and line with baking paper. **2** Preheat the oven to 160°C/gas 3. **3** In a bowl using a wooden spoon, or in a food processor, cream the butter with half the sugar, the vanilla seeds and lemon zest until pale and fluffy. **4** Whisk in the 8 egg yolks, one by one. **5** In a separate bowl mix together the olive oil and yogurt, then whisk into the butter cream mixture. **6** Sift together the flours and baking powder and whisk half into the mixture, then, when fully incorporated, whisk in the rest.

7 Now you need to make a meringue. **8** Preferably using a food mixer, whisk the 4 egg whites with the rest of the caster sugar until they form stiff peaks. **9** With a spatula, very gently fold into the butter, sugar and flour mixture, trying to keeping as much air in as possible. **10** Spoon into the cake tin and put into the preheated oven for around 1 hour, until springy to the touch. **11** Remove from the oven and from the tin. **12** Leave to cool on a wire rack, then slice horizontally in half or into thirds.

13 To make the cream, mix the sugar, cornflour and whipping cream in a bowl, then mix in the egg yolks. **14** Bring the milk to the boil in a small pan, then take off the heat and slowly whisk into the egg and sugar mixture. **15** Pour the mixture into a clean pan and whisk over a gentle heat until it comes to the boil, then turn down to a simmer for 1–2 minutes, whisking all the time until you have a custard consistency. **16** Transfer to a bowl, cover with clingfilm to prevent a skin forming, and leave to cool. **17** Sandwich the layers of cake together with the cream and/or jam and dust with icing sugar.

Makes 1 x 18cm cake

unsalted butter 250g, softened and cut into cubes, plus a little extra, for greasing the tin
caster sugar 300g
vanilla seeds from 1 pod
lemon zest of 1
eggs 4, separated
egg yolks 4
extra virgin olive oil 50g
plain yogurt 100g
plain flour 150g
cornflour 100g
baking powder 3 teaspoons
strawberry jam a little (optional)
icing sugar a little, for dusting

For the cream:
caster sugar 70g
cornflour 35g
whipping cream 100ml
egg yolks 5
full-fat milk 400ml

Gianduja chocolate cake

A chocolate cake should leave your mouth feeling full of the flavour of chocolate, not sugar, and this cake does that. Gianduja, the famous hazelnut chocolate from Piemonte, is the chocolate that I grew up with, so this is quite a nostalgic cake for me, and I must admit there are times when I think, forget the healthy breakfast, there is nothing better than a slice of this with a cappuccino, mid-morning.

There is such a huge choice of exciting, beautifully made chocolate available now, and that is what you want here.

Note: the ganache for this needs to be made 8 hours ahead.

1 To make the ganache, pour 75ml of the double cream into a pan, add the honey, and bring to the boil, then take off the heat. **2** Have the chocolate pieces in a bowl, and slowly whisk in the hot cream and honey mixture. **3** Whisk in the rest of the cream and put into the fridge for 8 hours before using.

4 Preheat the oven to 170°C/gas 3. **5** Grease a 24cm round cake tin, with a removable base, with a little butter and line with baking paper. **6** Put the cocoa powder into a bowl and pour in 120ml of hot water, slowly, mixing until smooth. **7** Stir in the buttermilk and keep to one side. **8** Separate the egg yolks from the whites. In a bowl, beat the egg yolks with the butter until pale and fluffy. **9** Fold in the flour, baking powder, bicarbonate of soda, vanilla seeds and salt, then fold in the reserved cocoa mixture. **10** Now you need to make a meringue. Preferably using a food mixer, whisk the egg whites with the sugar until they form stiff peaks. **11** With a spatula, very gently fold half the meringue into the cocoa mixture, keeping as much air in the mixture as possible, and when it is all incorporated, carefully fold in the rest. **12** Spoon the mixture into the tin and level it gently on top.

13 Put into the preheated oven and bake for 1 hour, until the centre springs back if you touch it with your fingertip. **14** Remove from the oven and leave to cool on a wire rack, placed over a tray or large plate, then split in half horizontally and spread with half the ganache. **15** Spread the rest of the ganache all over the top and sides of the cooled cake with a spatula.

Makes 1 x 24cm cake

good cocoa powder 40g	
buttermilk 120ml	
eggs 3	
unsalted butter 225g, softened and cut into cubes, plus a little extra for greasing the tin	
plain flour 240g	
baking powder 2 teaspoons	
bicarbonate of soda 1 teaspoon	
vanilla seeds from 1 pod	
fine salt ½ teaspoon	
caster sugar 200g	

For the gianduja ganache:

double cream 265ml	
clear honey 15g	
good gianduja chocolate 120g, broken into pieces	

Muffins

These are so easy to make, and so much more wholesome than anything you can buy in packets. You can omit the vanilla and instead add fruit, as you like: blueberries, raspberries, or sliced pear, apple or banana are all fantastic. If you are using a self-contained fruit like a berry, or even slices of banana, then you can add as much as 400g to the ingredients, but for a cut fruit like apple or pear which will release quite a bit of juice, I would keep it to 350g. Fold the fruit into the muffin mixture, just before putting into the moulds.

If you like you can turn the muffins into a dessert, adding some fresh fruit and a little whipped cream.

1 Have ready two 12-hole (medium) silicone moulds. **2** Preheat the oven to 180°C/gas 4. **3** In a bowl using a wooden spoon, or in a food processor, cream the butter, sugar, vanilla seeds, lemon zest and salt until pale and fluffy. **4** Whisk in the milk, a third at a time, making sure it is fully incorporated before each addition. **5** Lightly beat the eggs and egg yolks in a bowl, then whisk into the butter and sugar mixture a little at a time. **6** Mix the flour, baking powder and bicarbonate of soda together in a bowl, and whisk into the mixture. **7** Spoon into the moulds, filling each one three-quarters of the way to the top. **8** Put into the preheated oven and bake for 25 minutes, until risen and golden. **9** Remove, turn out and leave to cool on a wire rack.

Makes 24 medium muffins

unsalted butter	360g, softened and cut into cubes
caster sugar	400g
vanilla	seeds from 1 pod
lemon	zest of 1
fine salt	1 teaspoon
full-fat milk	500ml
eggs	4
egg yolks	3
plain flour	760g
baking powder	3 teaspoons
bicarbonate of soda	1 teaspoon

Apple crumble cake

This is so English, isn't it? The first time I ate apple crumble was when I was working at the Savoy and they used to make it in big trays, like school dinners, in the staff canteen. I really liked it, and so later Plaxy used to make it at home with custard. I don't remember when we first decided to turn it into a cake, but it still goes well with custard. Granny Smiths work well because they have an astringency and they hold their shape, unlike Bramleys, but Egremont Russets are also fantastic for this.

1 Preheat the oven to 160°C/gas 3. **2** First make the crumble: either combine the ingredients in a food mixer until they resemble breadcrumbs, or rub them together by hand, then put into the freezer for 30 minutes to keep the butter cold.

3 Grease a 24cm round cake tin (about 8cm deep), with a removable base, with a little butter and line with baking paper. **4** Peel, core and chop the apples. **5** In a bowl using a wooden spoon, or in a food processor, cream the butter, sugar and vanilla seeds until pale and fluffy. **6** Whisk in the eggs one by one, then whisk in the milk. **7** Sift the flour and baking powder together and fold into the mixture.
8 Mix in the apples. **9** Spoon into the cake tin, then take the crumble mixture from the freezer and spread over the top of the cake.
10 Bake in the preheated oven for 50 minutes, until golden on top. To check that it is ready, insert a skewer into the centre of the cake and it should come out clean. **11** Remove and cool on a wire rack, then dust with icing sugar.

Makes 1 x 24cm cake

Granny Smith apples 3

unsalted butter 110g, softened, plus a little extra for greasing the tin

caster sugar 180g

vanilla seeds from 1 pod

eggs 3

full-fat milk 150ml

plain flour 360g

baking powder 2 teaspoons

icing sugar a little for dusting

For the crumble:

unsalted butter 75g

caster sugar 75g

plain flour 75g

ground almonds 25g

ground cinnamon 2 teaspoons

289

Sicilian orange and chocolate cake

This is a very simple cake. You can use any really good juicy oranges, but Sicily is famous for its blood oranges, which are planted mainly over the plain of Catania and on the slopes of Mount Etna, so if you can find blood oranges in season this cake is even better; or you could substitute one of the oranges with a lemon or even a grapefruit, if you want to add an extra tang of citrus. Most Sicilian orange cakes are glazed with orange syrup, but I really like the extra dimension that comes from covering it with a crisp casing of dark chocolate.

1 Preheat the oven to 160°C/gas 3. **2** Grease a 24cm round cake tin, with a removable base, with a little butter and line with baking paper. **3** In a bowl using a wooden spoon, or in a food processor, cream the butter, sugar and orange zest in a bowl until pale and fluffy. **4** Whisk in the eggs one by one, then fold in the flour a little at a time, very gently, until it is all incorporated. **5** Spoon into the cake tin and bake in the preheated oven for 40 minutes, until golden and springy on top. **6** Remove from the oven and cool completely on a wire rack. Better still, put it into the fridge once it has cooled down, so that when you cover it with the chocolate glaze it will set really quickly.

7 To make the glaze, have the pieces of chocolate ready in a bowl. **8** Pour the cream and glucose into a pan and bring to the boil, then take off the heat and whisk into the chocolate. **9** Allow to cool for about 15 minutes, until just warm to the touch (if you have a kitchen thermometer, it should be 35°C). **10** Spread over the top and sides of the cake with a spatula.

Makes 1 x 24cm cake

unsalted butter 250g, softened and cut into cubes, plus a little extra for greasing the tin

caster sugar 250g

oranges or blood oranges, preferably Sicilian zest of 5

eggs 5

self-raising flour 250g, sifted

For the glaze:

good dark chocolate (at least 70 per cent cocoa solids) 200g, broken into pieces

whipping cream 150ml

liquid glucose 20g

Honey and vanilla roulade

This is another cake that makes a good dessert, with fruit, and owes its flavours to Sicily, where most of the confections centre around fresh ricotta and crystallised fruit.

1 Preheat the oven to 160°C/gas 3. **2** In a food mixer, mix the eggs, sugar, honey and vanilla on high speed until light and fluffy. **3** In a bowl sift the flour and baking powder and fold half into the egg and sugar mixture until it is all incorporated, then fold in the rest. **4** Line a large oven tray about 30cm x 40cm with baking paper and spread the mixture over the top. **5** Put into the preheated oven for 15 minutes until golden and springy to the touch. **6** Meanwhile, make the filling by whisking the ricotta and sugar together until fluffy. **7** Mix in the crystallised fruits. **8** Remove the sponge from the oven and turn out onto a fresh sheet of baking paper. While still hot, spread with the ricotta mixture and, lifting the baking paper to help you, roll it up like a Swiss roll. **9** Leave to cool before slicing.

Makes 1 roulade, enough for 4–6

eggs 5	
caster sugar 100g	
clear honey 1 tablespoon	
vanilla seeds from 1 pod	
plain flour 100g	
baking powder 2 teaspoons	

For the filling:

fresh ricotta 370g	
caster sugar 120g	
crystallised fruits 150g, chopped	

Apricot biscuits

These are so called because their shape resembles an apricot kernel. I really think we have to get back to baking simple biscuits like this which have six ingredients in them and take 15 minutes to bake, rather than buying something with three times as many ingredients, most of them put in to make the biscuits last a long time. All you need is an airtight tin and these will keep for up to a week. If you prefer, you can use raspberry or strawberry jam instead of apricot.

(see picture on next page)

1 Preheat the oven to 180°C/gas 4. **2** In a bowl whisk all the ingredients, except the jam, together. Ideally, put the mixture into a piping bag fitted with a large star nozzle. **3** Line a baking tray with baking paper and either pipe or spoon the mixture into shapes the size of an apricot kernel. Keep them well spaced apart. **4** Dot each one with a little jam. **5** Put into the preheated oven for 15 minutes until golden and firm. **6** Remove and cool, then dust with icing sugar.

Makes around 25–30 biscuits

unsalted butter 175g, very soft

icing sugar 60g, plus a little extra for dusting

plain flour 170g

cornflour 60g

full-fat milk 80ml

apricot jam 80g

Baci di cavaliere

We had some fun making these for the reception at the Italian Embassy when I was made a Cavaliere, the equivalent of a British knight, for services to gastronomy. Everybody jokingly said, 'Are you going to serve Ferrero Rocher?' referring to the famous nineties' TV advert about 'The Ambassador's Party' at which the guests were 'spoiled' by pyramids of the gold-wrapped hazelnut chocolates offered by a footman. So we thought, why not make our own version?

I have to take my hat off to the Ferrero family. Pietro Ferrero famously had a pastry shop in Alba in Piemonte in the forties when chocolate was scarce during the war, so he stretched what he had by mixing it into a paste with local hazelnuts and shaped it into loaves which could be sliced to eat on top of bread. In the fifties a creamier version was made and in the sixties Pietro's son Michele developed the recipe further, put it in jars and called it Nutella. Then in 1982 the family launched the chocolate and hazelnut confection, Ferrero Rocher.

Makes 30 baci

hazelnuts 30

dark chocolate (at least 70 per cent cocoa solids) 235g, cut into small pieces

whipping cream 220ml

unsalted butter 35g

For the coating:

hazelnuts 125g

dark chocolate (at least 70 per cent cocoa solids) 250g, cut into small pieces

cocoa butter 90g

1 Preheat the oven to 180°C/gas 4. Scatter all the hazelnuts, including those for the coating, over a baking tray and roast for about 8 minutes until golden. **2** Have the chocolate pieces ready in a bowl. **3** Bring 125ml of the cream to the boil in a pan, then take off the heat and pour over the chocolate, whisking until smooth. **4** Mix in the rest of the cream. **5** Leave to cool down until just warm to the touch (35°C if you have a kitchen thermometer), then whisk in the butter and put into the fridge until cold. **6** Divide into 30 pieces. **7** Push a hazelnut into each one and roll it so that the nut is completely encased. **8** Place the balls on a baking tray and put into the freezer while you make the coating.

9 For the coating, first finely crush the rest of the hazelnuts. **10** Put the chocolate and cocoa butter into a bowl and sit it over a pan of simmering water, making sure the bottom of the bowl doesn't touch the water. **11** When melted, remove from the heat, stir and mix in the crushed hazelnuts. **12** Take the chocolate balls from the freezer and dip each one into the chocolate and hazelnut mixture until completely coated. Lay on a tray or large plate lined with baking paper and keep in the fridge until ready to eat.

Baci di dama

We made these to go with the *baci di cavaliere* on page 295. In Italy, we have a tradition of calling little sweet things *baci* (kisses). Some of my favourites when I was growing up were *baci Perugina*, made with gianduja (chocolate and hazelnut) coating a whole hazelnut, which came in silver paper wrappers with blue stars, and had little love messages inside. And I always loved *baci di dama* (lady's kisses), which our cousins, the Gnocchis, made at their pastry shop in Gallarate. Traditionally they are made with tiny hazelnut biscuits sandwiched together with chocolate, but we make them entirely with chocolate.

1 In a bowl using a wooden spoon, or in a food processor, cream together all the ingredients, except for the dark chocolate, until smooth. **2** Put into the fridge for 30 minutes, covered with a clean cloth, to firm up. **3** Preheat the oven to 180°C/gas 4. **4** Take teaspoons of the chilled dough at a time, and roll into balls. **5** Line a baking tray with baking paper and lay the balls on top, pressing them down lightly to flatten them at the base. **6** Put into the preheated oven and bake for 20 minutes until firm. **7** Remove from the oven and allow to cool down. **8** Put the chocolate into a bowl and sit it over a pan of simmering water, making sure the bottom of the bowl doesn't touch the water. **9** When melted, transfer it to a piping bag and allow it to cool down to room temperature. **10** Take pairs of biscuits, pipe a little chocolate on to the base of one and sandwich the other on top. The biscuits will keep for a few days in an airtight tin.

Makes around 40 biscuits

plain flour 250g

unsalted butter 200g, softened

ground almonds 150g

caster sugar 200g

cocoa powder 20g

dark chocolate (at least 70 per cent cocoa solids) 50g, cut into small pieces

Ice creams and sorbets
x 4

When I was growing up, everyone went out to have ice cream. It was a social thing: families would eat together at home in the evening, then walk down to the gelateria, which was sometimes also a bar where the old men used to have a wine glass with a scoop of vanilla ice cream and a shot of whisky or brandy over the top. I remember nagging my grandad to let me have a taste of his. And I still love that idea whenever I go to Italy. But I also enjoy the idea of making a fresh cream with good eggs and fresh fruit, then turning on the ice-cream maker while you have your dinner and 25–30 minutes later you will have a beautiful fresh ice cream for dessert. I have even made ice cream with fresh fruit from the market and some lime juice on holiday using only a rough recipe in my head, and taken it down to the kids on the beach in the bucket of the ice-cream maker, with a handful of spoons. I have also included a recipe for coffee ice cream made with whole coffee beans, so it stays white. This is one to fool your friends, who will think they are about to eat a vanilla ice cream, and then be surprised by the unexpected coffee flavour.

These recipes are different to the ice creams we make at Locanda, where we have to use a complex chemistry of sugars in order to produce ice cream that can stay in the freezer for two weeks and every time we bring it out it will have a beautiful soft texture. The recipes here are simpler, and will work in any home ice-cream maker; however, they are designed to be eaten straight away, or be put into the freezer for a day only, then brought out to soften for a few minutes before eating. Any longer in the freezer, their texture will change and they will lose their creamy consistency and become rock hard. The sorbets are a little different, as you can keep them in the freezer if you like, and if you want to turn them into a granita, take them out and break them up with a fork a few times.

In all these recipes, which make enough for 6, the exact ratios are important, which is why I suggest you weigh everything, even the liquids and especially the eggs, as they vary in size so much.

White coffee ice cream

1 The night before, whisk 420g of full-fat milk in a pan with 210g of single cream, 110g of egg yolks (roughly 2–3 eggs), 150g of caster sugar and 20g of coffee beans. **2** Bring to just under the boil, but don't let it actually boil, or the cream will split. If you have a sugar thermometer, the temperature should be 84°C. **3** When the sugar has completely dissolved, take the pan off the heat. **4** Cool down, then put into the fridge until completely cold – if you want a more intense coffee flavour, leave it for up to 24 hours. **5** Take out the coffee beans and discard them. **6** Churn the cream in an ice-cream maker and eat straight away.

Chocolate ice cream

1 The night before, whisk 420g of full-fat milk, 200g of single cream, 110g of egg yolks (roughly 2-3 eggs), 145g of caster sugar and 40g of good cocoa powder (at least 70 per cent cocoa solids) in a pan. **2** Bring to just under the boil, but don't let it actually boil, or the cream will split. If you have a sugar thermometer, the temperature should be 84°C. **3** When the sugar has completely dissolved, take the pan off the heat. **4** Leave to cool down, then put into the fridge until completely cold. **5** Churn the cream in an ice-cream maker and eat straight away.

Vanilla ice cream

1 The night before, whisk 380g of full-fat milk in a pan with 205g of single cream, 110g of egg yolks (roughly 2–3 eggs),100g of caster sugar and 1 large vanilla pod (split and seeds scraped in). **2** Bring to just under the boil, but don't let it actually boil, or the cream will split. If you have a sugar thermometer, the temperature should be 84°C. **3** When the sugar has completely dissolved, take the pan off the heat. **4** Cool, then put into the fridge until completely cold. **5** Take out the vanilla pod. **6** Churn the cream in an ice-cream maker and eat straight away.

Strawberry sorbet

1 Bring 140g of water and 160g of caster sugar to just under the boil in a pan (84°C if you have a sugar thermometer). **2** When the sugar has completely dissolved, take off the heat, leave to cool and put into the fridge. **3** When completely cold, with a hand blender, or using a food processor, blend in 400g of hulled, fresh ripe strawberries. **4** Churn in an ice-cream maker and eat straight away.

Mango sorbet

1 Bring 260g of water and 140g of caster sugar to just under the boil in a pan (84°C if you have a sugar thermometer). **2** When the sugar has completely dissolved, take off the heat, leave to cool and put into the fridge. **3** When completely cold, with a hand blender, or using a food processor, blend in 400g of fresh mango. **4** Churn in an ice-cream maker and eat straight away.

Lemon sorbet

As this has no added fruit, we add some egg white, which helps to keep the sugar from crystallising.

1 Bring 255g of water and 255g of caster sugar to just under the boil in a pan (84°C if you have a sugar thermometer) with the peel of a whole lemon. **2** When the sugar has completely dissolved, take off the heat, leave to cool and put into the fridge. **3** When completely cold, add 250g of lemon juice and 35g of egg white. **4** Remove the peel and churn the sorbet in an ice-cream maker and eat straight away.

Almond ice cream

1 The night before, whisk 470g of almond milk in a pan with 200g of single cream, 110g of egg yolks (roughly 2–3 eggs), 80g of demerara sugar and 50g of icing sugar. **2** Bring to just under the boil, but don't let it actually boil, or the cream will split. If you have a sugar thermometer, the temperature should be 84°C. **3** When the sugar has completely dissolved, take the pan off the heat. **4** Cool, then put into the fridge until completely cold. **5** Churn in an ice-cream maker and eat straight away.

Melon sorbet

1 Bring 245g of water and 145g of caster sugar to just under the boil in a pan (84°C if you have a sugar thermometer). **2** When the sugar has completely dissolved, take off the heat, leave to cool and put into the fridge. **3** When completely cold, with a hand blender, or using a food processor, blend in 410g of fresh ripe melon pieces. **4** Churn in an ice-cream maker and eat straight away.

Gorgonzola panna cotta

Panna cotta is one of those easy desserts that you can make really quickly if you have friends coming around to eat. Pop it into the fridge, and by the time you have eaten your main course it will be chilled and ready. This recipe, served with chocolate 'crumble', plays with the idea of chocolate and salt. We put just a little sweet Gorgonzola (*dolce*) into the panna cotta mixture – this is the young, soft, rich and creamy version of the famous cheese from my region of Lombardy which, despite being called sweet, adds a touch of saltiness that goes really well with the chocolate. I like it also with some slices of fresh, juicy pear.

1 Soak the gelatine leaf in cold water for a few minutes until softened, then squeeze out the water. **2** Bring the cream, sugar and Gorgonzola to the boil in a pan, then take off the heat and stir in the gelatine until it dissolves. **3** Divide the mixture between 8 ramekins and leave to cool, then put into the fridge for 3–4 hours to set.

4 If making the chocolate crumble, preheat the oven to 160°C/gas 3. **5** Put all the ingredients into a food processor and mix just enough to create a crumble – don't overwork it or it will become pasty. **6** Spread over a baking tray and put into the preheated oven for 15 minutes, then remove from the oven and when cool enough to touch, break up any clumps, so you have a quite even crumble. **7** Turn out the panna cotta onto plates and serve with some pears, and chocolate crumble, if you like.

Serves 8

gelatine 1 leaf
whipping cream 250ml
caster sugar 45g
sweet Gorgonzola 45g

For the chocolate crumble (optional):
plain flour 100g
good cocoa powder 30g
ground almonds 50g
demerara sugar 100g
cornflour 25g
baking powder 1 teaspoon
unsalted butter 110g, softened

To serve (optional):
ripe pears 4, cored and sliced

Index

Acknowledgments

First, but in no particular order, a big thank you to Louise Haines at 4th Estate, who really believed I could do another book, and with her faith and good-natured badgering, we have finally got there. Lisa Linder, not only for her great eye and beautiful photography, but also her infectious enthusiasm, boundless energy and constantly cheerful disposition that kept us all going to get that 'final shot' when we wanted to pack everything away. Sheila Keating, who once again spun all my billions of spoken words together seamlessly, and Sam Wolfson, who designed her great big heart out under duress, and listened to everyone's many opinions without getting flustered.

Plaxy, who is my silent and faceless backbone and partner, who gets none of the credit, but is in fact always in the background, making the decisions, whilst I am the show pony. Dita (Margherita), my beautiful, clever daughter whose incredible resilience in the face of adversity has made me realise that you can achieve whatever you put your mind to. Jack Exton, of whom I am also immeasurably proud, who has become my moral compass: talented, kind and funny. If I need an honest opinion on a new dish that I can trust, he is my go-to. My mother Giuseppina, and my father, Ferruccio who made me and Mara Exton, my beloved mother-in-law, who has always believed in me.

Rino Bono for being the 'Real Sicilian Man', whose strength and silent unwavering loyalty have been inspirational to all the young chefs who have passed through the kitchen in the last 15 years. Our rock: thank you Rino. Roberto Veneruzzo, a member of my family: for who you are and who you have become. Nikki Morris who has risen from a little girl to a magnificent woman; Giulia Muccio for being one of the family; Daniele Solimando; Costanzo Capella; Simone Bottaro, our own personal 007; and Toni Barone. And under the watchful eye of Vacaba Cisse – The Real Man – are Bangalay Sanogo, Jonathan Ronyl Mbounou and Rabin Claude. Thanks guys; Kings, each and every one of you. Sergio Iacono – tough and talented. Sergio and Faa (Jidaphak Praneebut) Fontana: how can we thank you enough? Simone Devoti for his enthusiasm, talent and good nature, and Linda Vittoni and Irene Forni – realising my pastry dreams.

Katie Osborne, our clever, exotic wonder woman, whose incredible good grace and knack for assessing every situation correctly has made daily irritations and dilemmas vanish. How on earth did we cope before you? Hayley Loughran, for putting up with me (and our dog Olive) and making my day an altogether smoother machine. Oh, and overcoming the fear of making travel reservations. Marco Arrigo for his friendship and tireless enthusiasm for all things coffee. Actually, just all things.

Frankie Unsworth, who managed the unenviable cutlery-counting job after the mess of a big boozy lunch without complaint and brought great plates to the table – literally. And talking of plates, many thanks to ceramicist Owen Wall and Very Good & Proper; thanks, too, to Linea Casa. Dominica Stanczyk, a smiley efficient whirlwind with a knack for bubble-wrapping anything that stands still for longer than 30 seconds, and Laura Huhta for clever photographic witchery; Sarah Thickett, for keeping everything on track, and Louise Tucker, a truly safe pair of hands who guided the book to the finish line. Annie Lee, for her diligent copy-editing; and Alice Saunders at LAW who has made the whole process seamless.

Emily Dormer and Stanley Needham for making sure I don't seize up entirely and bringing Stan the man to cheer us all up. Nigel Wilson for his enormous heart and brilliant eye; Elio Resta, Ian Black, Richard Howell (sandbag it!), Carl and all the Nardo gang for introducing us to another way of living. Athena McAlpine and Pierluigi for always making us so welcome at the truly fabulous Il Convento; Roy Ackerman and Adrian Gill, both of whom gave me strength and encouragement from day one. The world is a much greyer place without the pair of you.

Willie for his magical chocolate, Roccbox for their wonderful portable cooking station; Agnelli for the beautiful pots and pans that make what I do at home and work that bit more enjoyable; Graham Barnard from Matrix Kitchen, who has guided us through the years with his incredible knowledge – if there's anything he doesn't know about kitchens, then it isn't worth knowing. Gaggenau, and in particular Stephen Brownless, who made it possible to achieve my dream kitchen. Not once but twice.

Then the gang: Andy (is that my lighter?) Needham; Clem 'the Pope' Arricale; Valerio Daros; Andrea Cirino; Max Folli; Dixie and Charles Tashima; Rebecca and Damon; Paul and Serena; Antonio Carluccio; Simon and Mel; Salvo and Elisa Sardo and the doubly delicious Aurora; Michele Righetto; Paolo Ciabatti; David Buxton and Lynn; Antonio Alfano; Carlo Caporicci, for your friendship and wonderful truffles; Franco and Ann Taruschio; Joost Verhoeff, my beautiful friend in Delft; Virgilio Gennaro; Zane McGill at Dragon Smoke; Jacqueline Drewe at Curtis Brown, who has made painful things a pleasure. And no thanks to Dinos Chapman whatsoever. For anything.